OFF THE SHELF
and
INTO YOURSELF

This book is designed for your personal reading pleasure and profit. It is also designed for group study. A leader's guide, with visual aids (Son-Power Multiuse Transparency Masters) and Rip-Offs (student activity booklets) are available from your local Christian bookstore or from the publisher.

A one-day seminar based on the material presented in *Off the Shelf and into Yourself* is also available. For more information on how your church or organization can sponsor a Personal Spiritual Growth Seminar, contact the authors at Media Ministries, 516 East Wakeman, Wheaton, Ill. 60187, (312/665-4594).

OFF THE SHELF
and
INTO YOURSELF

Getting more from God's Word

Terry Hall
WITH KAREN HALL

VICTOR BOOKS

a division of SP Publications, Inc.

WHEATON ILLINOIS 60187

Offices also in Fullerton. California • Whitby. Ontario. Canada • Amersham-on-the-Hill. Bucks. England

MIDLAND CHRISTIAN CENTRE
BOOKSHOP ● *RESOURCES*
322 GT EASTERN HWY. Phone 274 6737
(P.O. Box 97, MIDLAND 6056)

Library of Congress Catalog Number: 81-86103
ISBN: 088207-589-6

To Bob and Bev Kerns . . .
super encouragers
and
special friends.

Contents

1

The Bible and You

Nobody can say I didn't try. I was old enough to go to high school, but I was only a baby in the Christian faith—and I wanted to grow. The problem was that lots of people told me "you need to study the Bible," but nobody really taught me how. So I tried the potluck approach—flipping through the Bible looking for a quick emotional lift to keep the devil away. Sometimes I got a blessing, but mostly I just got bored.

My attempt to read through the Bible for the first time was a letdown too. Genesis rocked along OK with the four big events of chapters 1—11: Creation, Fall, Flood, and Babel. The four great men of Genesis 12—50 (Abraham, Isaac, Jacob, and Joseph) were interesting too.

I stuck with Exodus through the 10 plagues and the Red Sea wipeout. Then I came to the part about the tabernacle and got jammed up reading about all the boards, bolts, and bars. So I skipped over to Leviticus, which made even less sense to me. My read-through-the-Bible program died right there.

Because I wasn't getting enough out of God's Word on my own, I became more and more dependent on other people (preachers, Sunday School teachers, etc.) to tell me what the Bible had to say. I learned some things that way. But I missed out on the fun of personally discovering Bible truth. It was kind of like giving my girl-friend's unopened love letters to another guy, then letting him read and interpret them for me.

In spite of my frustrations, I did make some progress in the faith. I even started speaking at some of our high school Bible club meetings. But that created another kind of problem.

Have you ever seen the inside of a water pipe that's been used in a home for 15 to 20 years? Even though the water flowing through the pipe is supposed to be clean, the pipe can become completely sealed off with residue.

In preparing my Bible club messages, I was coming to God's Word in an impersonal way, letting it flow through me to others like water through a pipe. But I wasn't allowing the Word to work on *me* first. And, as a result, I was getting clogged up inside.

Psalm 1 indicates that God's people are to be like *trees* (not pipes). As trees planted by God's "rivers of living water," we need to sink our roots deep into the subsoil of Scripture. As Bible truth comes up daily to nourish our minds, emotions, and wills, it *changes* us. Then our changed lives, not just our nice-sounding words, can be the message we share with others.

One of my biggest problems with the Bible was lack of time for it. I needed to learn how to rear-range my *priorities*. Priorities are simply those things that are most important to us. They are what we choose to do first with our time.

I've since learned that carving out quality time

ROOTED iN GOD'S WORD

for God is more a matter of the *heart* than the head. It's a love affair. No one has to tell me to spend good gulps of my week with the girl I love. On my first date with Karen, my mind, emotions, and will took counsel together and decided to get to know her better. That decision led to four years of going together and now 17 years of marriage.

But what about God and His love letters written in the Bible to us? Somewhere, sometime we have to decide whether we really want to know Him better. The more we get to know Him, the more we will love Him. The more we love Him, the more we will want to spend time with Him.

I wish I had learned sooner how to make spending time with God a priority. I wish someone had taught me how to use my Bible and get something out of it. And for every time someone told me to study the Bible, I wish I had been shown how to "feed myself."

What's in It for You?

That's what this book is all about—practical ways to feed yourself on God's Word and grow faster as a result. A few of the benefits of applying these methods are:

- Bible study can become a joy instead of a pain;
- you can understand what you read in the Bible;
- you can experience the fun of personally discovering Bible truth;
- you can find God's will for your life;
- you can fall in love with the Bible's Author.

How Do You Rate?

How would you rate on the following confidential checkup?

- Do I usually read the Bible and pray each day?
- Which of the following are my greatest obstacles to consistent personal Bible study?

_____ I don't have time.

_____ I don't know how.

_____ There's no quiet place at my house.

_____ I don't understand the Bible well enough.

_____ I have never developed the habit.

- Have I ever taken a course or had any instruction in how to study the Bible on my own?

● Have I ever read any books on the subject (other than the one I am now reading)?

If you find yourself suffering from spiritual irregularity, you're not alone! One survey found that only 12 percent of the people who say they believe the Bible actually read it every day; 34 percent read it only once a week; and 42 percent hardly ever read it. That leaves 12 percent of those claiming to believe the Bible who *never* read it!

Is Anything Sticking Upstairs?

If you are a Bible reader, how much are you really learning? Try these questions on for size:
● What is the second book in the Bible?
● Which is the last book of the Bible?
● Who wrote most of the Psalms?
● Who authored 13 of the New Testament books?
● Which Bible book tells the history of the early church (its spread from Jerusalem to Rome)?
● Name any one of the sons of Jacob.
● Name any one of the kings of Israel or Judah.
● Name any one of the Old Testament prophets.
● Quote the first of the Ten Commandments.
● Who was a missionary companion of the Apostle Paul?
● Quote one of the Beatitudes.
● Who was the brother of Mary and Martha? (Hint: Jesus raised him from the dead.)
● What is the fourth Gospel?
● Quote the Golden Rule.
For answers to the above, consult the Bible.

Why Bother?

So what if people don't know much about the Bible? Why study the Bible anyway?

• For one thing, it is the only way to get an accurate and honest view of ourselves. The Bible is like a mirror that reflects our strengths and weaknesses from God's viewpoint (James 1:23-25).

• The Bible *builds faith* in us as we read and hear it (Romans 10:17).

• Only through believing God's Word can we be *born again spiritually* (1 Peter 1:23).

• The "Sword of the Spirit," God's Word, is our *defense against Satan* (Ephesians 6:16-17).

• God's Word gives us *guidance* (Psalm 119:105),

THE BIBLE IS LIKE a MIRROR

HOLY BIBLE

protection from sin (Psalm 119:11), *cleansing* (Psalm 119:9), and a means of *spiritual growth* (1 Peter 2:2).

Why study the Bible? One other important reason is that God tells us to study it: "Do your best to present yourself to God as one approved, a workman who does not need to be ashamed and who correctly handles the Word of truth" (2 Timothy 2:15).

When God tells us to do something, it is always for our benefit. Second Timothy 3:16-17 lists four benefits the Bible can give us (if we let it): "All Scripture is God-breathed and is useful for teaching, rebuking, correcting, and training in righteousness, so that the man of God may be thoroughly equipped for every good work."

(1) Teaching. God gave the Bible to teach us the faith. His Word gives a basis for our beliefs.

(2) Rebuking. Studying the Bible exposes the false philosophies and wrong ideas we pick up in the world.

(3) Correcting. This benefit involves resetting the direction of our lives. God's Word shows us where we are going astray. Like a good surgeon, the Bible may sometimes have to hurt in order to heal.

(4) Training in righteousness. Studying the Bible shows us the right way to live. The ultimate result is that we may be people of God who are fully equipped for every good work God has for us (v. 17). Through the power of God and His Word in us, we can be winners in life!

God tells us to study the Bible also because our spiritual growth depends on it. "Like newborn babes, long for the pure milk of the Word, that by it you may grow in respect to salvation" (1 Peter 2:2, NASB).

Just as physical babies need milk to grow, spiritual babies need the nourishment of God's Word. The amazing thing is that as we grow up in God, the same Book that gave us our spiritual baby food also provides our T-bone steaks. It's impossible to outgrow the Bible, just as it's impossible to grow without it!

"I Tried It Before"

Maybe you have tried before to get into God's Word, and it didn't work. You didn't grow into a spiritual giant. In fact, you couldn't tell that Bible study did you much good at all.

Part of the problem may be a need to learn some *how-to's* of Bible study. This book can help with that area. But another thing to remember is, spiritual growth doesn't happen instantly.

It was quite an experience to go to my wife Karen's high school class reunion. Everyone looked older except her! It's hard for anyone to notice the little daily changes. But they're happening. And 5, 10, or 20 years of those little daily changes add up!

A basic principle runs all through the Bible: *light obeyed brings more light; light rejected brings darkness.* As we walk in the light God gives us for today, we'll get more light when we need it.

The key is to be faithful to *obey* the little insights God gives us. Jesus promises that a person who is faithful in little will be made ruler over much. (See Matthew 25:21.)

God promises that regular study of His Word will have long-term benefits. "But we all, with unveiled face beholding as in a mirror the glory of the Lord, are being transformed into the same image from glory to glory, just as from the Lord, the Spirit" (2 Corinthians 3:18, NASB).

As we regularly see the Lord's glory (all that is beautiful and good about Him) reflected to us in the divine mirror (God's Word), the Holy Spirit changes us into the image we see!

God can work major changes in us instantly if He chooses. And sometimes He does. But more often He changes us through the routine of daily faithfulness.

He could do it all by Himself if He wanted, without any effort on our part. But He has chosen our cooperation as part of the growth process. We do what we can do, and He does all we can't do. Moses stretched his rod over the Red Sea; God had to part the waters. Joshua marched his troops around Jericho; God had to make the city walls collapse.

We can read the Bible; God has to make it come alive for us. We can study it; God has to open our understanding. When we do our part, God is ready, willing, and able to do His part.

This Book: How to Use It

The following chapters explain a variety of methods for getting into God's Word (and getting the Word into you). All of these methods are organized around *five levels of approaching the Bible:* reading, studying, memorizing, meditating, and applying.

(1) **Reading the Bible.** Chapters 2 and 3 tell how Bible reading can become more meaningful—and enjoyable.

18

(2) **Studying the Bible.** Chapters 4-9 tell how to dig deeper into God's Word and uncover its treasures.

(3) **Memorizing the Bible.** Chapter 10 gives eight techniques for stopping the "great brain drain."

(4) **Meditating on the Bible.** Chapter 11 tells how to bridge the gap between belief and behavior.

(5) **Applying the Bible.** Chapter 12 deals with how to respond to Bible promises and commands (how much to do yourself and how much to leave for God to do).

Don't expect to master all five levels immediately. And feel free to skip around, trying out the methods that interest you most. If you are studying this book in a class or small group, try to catch on to each method as it is presented. Then start using the methods you like best in your own Bible time. However you use this book, make sure you use *the* Book—God's Word—along with it.

Don't forget that the Holy Spirit is the One who makes the Bible come alive. Start your Bible times by praying, "Open my eyes to see wonderful things in Your Word" (Psalm 119:18, LB). With the Holy Spirit's help, the methods discussed in this book can help you get more out of God's Word.

2

The Big Picture

Dave and Chrissy were whispering to each other and holding hands across the aisle. A fifth spitball had just rocketed by. And the substitute teacher was trying to figure out who kept making the frog sounds—*ribit, rribit . . . rrribit!* As soon as she eyed a likely suspect, another "frog" would sound off from another part of the classroom.

Jenny tried for the fourth time to read page 189 of her English book. But the words marched across the page and flitted away—barely in sight, definitely out of mind. So she closed her book and counted the dandruff flakes on the back of Seymour Pflug's shirt.

Similar problems can occur when we try to read the Bible. Even with few distractions, the tendency is to see without really reading. Our eyes pass over the page, but we just see words on paper. It's all too easy to put on mental water skis and skim through the water of the Word. But we miss so much in the process.

Another problem is *aimless reading*, not having any particular goal in mind other than "putting in our time." If we aim at nothing, we'll usually hit it.

Do you ever feel like you are reading more and remembering less? Have you ever reread a Bible passage, and realized you were really "reading" it for the first time? There is a solution!

On the surface, this method for getting more out of Bible reading sounds so simple that you may wonder how it will help. But it is one of the most valuable and exciting things Karen and I have ever done with the Bible.

Putting the Mind in Gear

To get more out of Bible reading, come up with an *original chapter title* for every chapter you read. The idea is to read one chapter carefully (and more than once, if necessary) till you can boil down the main idea to a few words.

Making a chapter title is like writing a newspaper headline. A chapter title, like a headline, should be to-the-point and capture the most important idea.

Not only will this method help you get a lot more from every chapter you read, it will also give you a grip on God's *big ideas.* Each Bible chapter is like a suitcase full of tools for a happy and successful life. Chapter titles are like the handles and identification tags. Eventually, your titles can become your index to the whole tool collection.

One reason people don't read the Bible is that it seems too long and complex. But imagine a list of chapter titles which you have developed for a single book in the Bible. A quick look at your list could remind you, within seconds, of what that book is about.

Also, as you are reading through a Bible book, you can quickly review the chapters you've read up to that point just by checking your list of chapter titles. The Bible won't seem nearly so complicated when you put handles on the big ideas.

F-O-U-R

The following four guidelines are recommended for successful chapter titling:

> **F**our words or less.
> **O**riginal to you.
> **U**nique to that chapter.
> **R**etainable for the big idea(s).

Four words in each chapter title is the limit. Such a limit forces you to think harder about the chapter. Also, using a few words makes it easier to remember the big ideas. But if a chapter can be summarized in one, two, or three words, fine! You don't have to use all four.

Original means the chapter title is the product of your own incredible mental capacities. Sure, reference Bibles are available with all the chapters already titled. But those titles belong to the editor. He got the blessing of creating them. In chapter titling, it's your *own* thought that counts!

For getting into the Bible on this first level—the *reading* level—it's best to use a Bible without extra notes and study helps. These have their place, as we'll see in chapter 4.

Unique means that a title fits *one particular* chapter of the Bible. For example, "God Speaks to Man" is too general a title. It could fit most of the Bible's 1,189 chapters!

Retainable means the title helps you recall the major idea(s) of the chapter. Sometimes it would be easy to find a well-known verse and make that your title. But that one verse might be only a minor part of what the chapter is about.

Good titles don't have to be profound. I titled Ephesians 1, "Redemption by the Trinity." I feel that's an appropriate title for the only Bible chapter completely devoted to the work of the Father, Son, and Holy Spirit in our salvation. My title for Nehemiah 1, "Report and Response," sounds humdrum. But the chapter is about (1) the report given to Nehemiah concerning Jerusalem's broken-down walls, and (2) his prayerful and tearful response.

Taming the Tough Ones

What happens when you have read the chapter once and can't think of a title? Sometimes the solution is to read the chapter again. The Lord doesn't mind!

I used to think the important thing was to keep moving, especially when I was trying to read through the whole Bible. But as important as it is to read through the Bible (or even a single Bible book), it's even more crucial to *get something* out of what you read.

What else can you do if a chapter just seems too long or complex for one good four-word title? One trick is to title the *major sections* of the chapter first. This helps break down a complex chapter into bite-size ideas. The next step is to combine the titles of the major sections into one chapter title. For example, James 1 has three major sections. Titles could be:

verses 1-11: External Trials to Test
verses 12-18: Internal Temptations to Sin
verses 19-27; Hearing Plus Doing Word

Combining these three titles, a suitable chapter title for James 1 could be "Trials, Temptations, Doing Word." These four words capture the three big ideas of the chapter. (Note that a title doesn't have to be a sentence, and that small connecting words ["a," "and," "the"] can be omitted.)

Taking time to title the major divisions of a chapter is more work. But getting into God's Word is like banking: The greater your investment, the greater your interest!

Now try making your own title for Jonah, chapter 1.

I simply call it "Jonah Runs from God." What do you call it? Did you find you read the chapter more carefully since you were looking for the big idea(s)?

Some chapters are harder to title than others.

But I guarantee that every one of the Bible's 1,189 chapters can be titled. I've done it, and so have many other people.

But don't get overwhelmed by the idea of titling all 1,189. Start with a single Bible book. Do a chapter a day in Ephesians, for example, and you will title the whole book in 6 days. You can do Romans in 16 days, or Genesis in 50.

You may want to write your titles in the margins of your Bible. Or list them in a notebook. Later, when you read the same chapters again, you can review and revise your original titles.

Right now, for practice, title the rest of Jonah. (It only has three more chapters.) Then take on a longer Bible book.

Here's how one teen titled Jonah:

Chapter 1: Jonah Runs from God

Chapter 2: Jonah Prays from Fish

Chapter 3: Jonah Preaches in Nineveh
Chapter 4: Jonah Pouts over Repentance
Your titles will be different, of course, since you
want to be original!

Plugging in Permanently

Titling Bible chapters will help you understand
what you read and help you get more out of it.
Titling will help you get a grip on God's big
ideas—in a chapter, a book, or the whole Bible.

A variation of the chapter titling method can
help you *remember* the big ideas. This method uses
something called an *acrostic*. To make an acrostic,
you lay out a word vertically, letting each letter of
the word start another word or thought:

God's
Riches
At
Christ's
Expense

Or:

Forsaking
All
I'll
Trust
Him

To make an acrostic of a Bible book, you need a
word, phrase, or sentence which has the same
number of letters as the book has chapters. Also,
the acrostic word should in some way express
what the book is about.

In Jonah, for example, what four-letter word

comes to mind as one of the "largest" things in the book? *Fish*, of course. So, your Jonah titles could be restated:

Flight from God's Call (chapter 1)
Intercession from within Fish (chapter 2)
Salvation of Nineveh's People (chapter 3)
Humbling of Pouting Prophet (chapter 4)

Try restating your own titles to fit a different acrostic word for Jonah. There are lots of other four-letter themes in the book, such as *obey, worm, call, city, Lord, flee, pray,* or *fear*. One fish fan did Jonah this way:

Jonah Runs from God
Anxious Prayer of Repentance
Warning Nineveh of Destruction
Sulking Prophet Taught Compassion

Longer books can become acrostic *sentences*, like "JOHN, THE GOSPEL OF BELIEF" (21 letters for John's 21 chapters). Or, "JOB, GOD'S SUFFERING SERVANT, IS TESTED AND RESTORED" (42 letters for the 42-chapter Book of Job).

Barry Did It

A young man named Barry Huddleston has titled every chapter in the Bible as an acrostic, and had his work published. Not surprisingly, Barry's book is called *The Acrostic Bible*. (See the page sample on page 28.)

While he was a college student, Barry got so excited about this project that he spent 80 hours one spring vacation working on it! He claims that titling the Bible's chapters and restating them in acrostics drew him closer to the Lord than anything else he's done with the Bible.

GENESIS

(You can get a copy of *The Acrostic Bible* at a Christian bookstore or order it by sending $5 to: Media Ministries, 516 East Wakeman, Wheaton, IL 60187.)

You Choose

Chapter titling the whole Bible in acrostics isn't your thing? Fine. You may want to stick with the basic titling method described in the first part of this chapter. Or you might want to try the following variations on the acrostic method. It's your decision.

But remember, *variety* adds spice to Bible reading. Get acquainted with several different methods, then use the ones that work for you.

Here are two more variations on the acrostic titling method:

(1) Make your Bible chapter titles all start with the *same letter*. Here's how you might title the Book of Jonah:

Running from God (chapter 1)
Repentance in Fish (chapter 2)
Revival in Nineveh (chapter 3)
Remorse in Suburbs (chapter 4)

(2) Make a book's titles all *sound alike*, rhyming on the first word. Here's an example using Jonah again:

RUNNING from God (chapter 1)
PRAYING in Fish (chapter 2)
WARNING in Nineveh (chapter 3)
POUTING outside City (chapter 4)

Hint: the easiest way to make the first words rhyme is to use words ending in "-ed," "-ing," or "-ion."

17 Action-advancing Books

Old Testament

Gen.	Exodus	Num.	Josh.	Judges	1 Sam.	2 Sam.	1 Kings	2 Kings	Babylon-ian Captivity	Ezra	Neh.
1	2	3	4	5	6	7	8	9		10	11

LEV. DEUT.   RUTH   1 CHRON. 2 CHRON.   ESTHER

JOB

PSALMS SONG
PROV.
ECC.

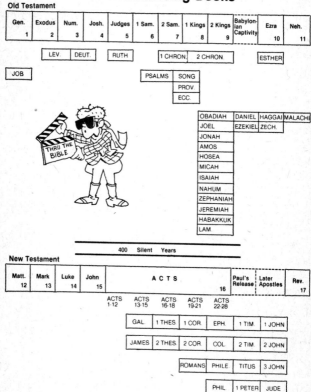

THRU THE BIBLE

OBADIAH DANIEL HAGGAI MALACHI
JOEL EZEKIEL ZECH.
JONAH
AMOS
HOSEA
MICAH
ISAIAH
NAHUM
ZEPHANIAH
JEREMIAH
HABAKKUK
LAM.

400   Silent   Years

New Testament

Matt.	Mark	Luke	John	ACTS					Paul's Release	Later Apostles	Rev.
12	13	14	15					16			17

ACTS 1-12   ACTS 13-15   ACTS 16-18   ACTS 19-21   ACTS 22-28

GAL. 1 THES. 1 COR. EPH. 1 TIM. 1 JOHN

JAMES 2 THES. 2 COR. COL. 2 TIM. 2 JOHN

ROMANS PHILE. TITUS 3 JOHN

PHIL. 1 PETER JUDE

2 PETER HEB.

Getting the Big Picture

Doing a detailed *study* of one section of the Bible provides a close-up view of that section. *Reading* large chunks of the Bible gives a broader view, a look at the big picture. Both studying and reading are important. Here's a reading shortcut to get that big picture into focus.

Did you know you can take in the entire *story* of the Bible by just reading 17 of its books? The story line doesn't flow continuously through all 66 books from Genesis to Revelation. The main action is contained in just 17 "action-advancing" books.

So, titling these 17 books first will give you a clear focus on the Bible's big picture. Then you can go back and read the other books. The chart on page 30 shows these 11 Old Testament and 6 New Testament books.

Notice that the rest of the Bible's 66 books are lined up under the book or time period they supplement. So, by reading everything in one of the vertical lists, you could read all the Scriptures about one period of history. For example, to read everything about the time of Ezra (who led the Jews home from the Babylonian Captivity), you would read the Book of Ezra, then Esther, Haggai, and Zechariah.

Here's a summary of the Bible through these 17 action-advancing books:

(1) GENESIS: Beginning of everything but God. After man's repeated rebellion, God begins to develop a Hebrew nation through Abraham, Isaac, Jacob, and Joseph. The Hebrews end up in Egypt.

(2) EXODUS: Hebrews delivered from Egypt and led by Moses to Mount Sinai. Commandments

are given plus directions for a portable worship center called the tabernacle.

(3) NUMBERS: Forty years' wandering in the wilderness for Hebrews' lack of belief in God's ability to lead them safely into the Promised Land.

(4) JOSHUA: Conquest and settlement of Hebrews in their Promised Land under General Joshua.

(5) JUDGES: Twelve Hebrew military deliverers who also ruled the Jews for a time.

(6) 1 SAMUEL: Samuel, the last of the judges, and Saul, the first Hebrew king.

(7) 2 SAMUEL: David, Hebrew king number two.

(8) 1 KINGS: Solomon, Hebrew king number three. Jewish nation splits north and south. Israel and Judah have rival kings.

(9) 2 KINGS: More rival kings of Israel and Judah till both Hebrew nations are conquered. Israel goes to Assyria; Judah to Babylon.

(10) EZRA: Zerubbabel and Ezra lead Hebrews home to Judah after 70 years in Babylonian captivity. Jewish temple rebuilt.

(11) NEHEMIAH: Rebuilding Jerusalem's walls. End of Old Testament. Next on the calendar are 400 "silent" years not recorded in Old or New Testament.

(12) MATTHEW: Life of Christ as King of the Jews.

(13) MARK: Life of Christ as Servant of all.

(14) LUKE: Life of Christ as Son of man.

(15) JOHN: Life of Christ as Son of God.

(16) ACTS: Start of the church and spread of the Gospel through the apostles' journeys to the then-known world.

(17) REVELATION: Letters to churches and

pre-written history of the great tribulation and Christ's kingdom to come.

That's the Bible story, which is really *His* story. Read it! And look for the Bible's big ideas, chapter by chapter.

3

Take Note

It was the Olsons' first big family vacation in years, and their first trip ever to Chicago. What a letdown it was to arrive by car on a rainy night and get lost while looking for their downtown hotel. But seeing the sun the next morning helped lift everyone's spirits.

They decided to begin their tour of Chicago by visiting the world's tallest building, the Sears Tower. They took an elevator to the top. And when they stepped out on the 101st-floor observation deck, they got an entirely different view of the city.

Below them was the magnificent panorama of Chicago, spread out in miniature. The city began to take shape in their minds with the help of a map and guidebook of major landmarks and attractions.

Once they got their bearings in all four directions, the Olsons took turns looking through a rental telescope. It was fun to start with the big picture, then zoom in on the little ones. As the Olsons took in the sights during the following days, that panoramic view from the tower helped keep all the different locations in perspective. Everything meant more because each family member could relate the little pieces of Chicago to the big picture.

When beginning a tour of a Bible book, it's also a good idea to start with a view from the top. Before diving deeply into the book to analyze its individual parts, spend some time getting the big picture of that book.

Choose a book of the Bible and read it straight through. It's best to read the whole book at a single sitting. This step is not as difficult as it may sound. Half of the books in the Bible are so short they would take up only two columns in an average newspaper. For longer books, use the chart on page 36 as a reading guide for breaking the bigger books into manageable parts.

Reading straight through once is good; reading through the book twice is better. Each reading will enrich your understanding.

Try to discover what the book, as a whole, is saying. One way to get this big picture in focus is to make your own chapter headings as described in chapter 2 of this book. A list of original chapter titles is like a skeleton—something very basic, but necessary! Once the skeleton is put together, the next step is to put some meat on those bones. How?

Get Out of Neutral

One of the best ways to "fill out" your understanding of a Bible passage is to form the habit of taking notes. It requires some extra effort, but that's part of the value. Searching out what God is

Bible Reading Guide

Read longer Bible books in sections, according to the following chapter groupings. (Shorter books are shown as single reading units.)

Genesis	1-11, 12-25, 26-36, 37-50	Matthew	1-11, 12-15, 16-28
		Mark	1-8, 9-16
Exodus	1-10, 11-18, 19-24, 25-40	Luke	1-8, 9-18, 19-24
		John	1-12, 13-21
Leviticus	1-10, 11-17, 18-27	Acts	1-7, 8-12, 13-21, 22-28
Numbers	1-10, 11-21, 22-36		
Deuteronomy	1-11, 12-16, 17-26, 27-34	Romans	1-8, 9-16
		1 Corinthians	1-10, 11-16
Joshua	1-12, 13-24	2 Corinthians	1-7, 8-13
Judges	1-9, 10-21	Galatians	1-6
Ruth	1-4	Ephesians	1-6
1 Samuel	1-8, 9-15, 16-31	Philippians	1-4
2 Samuel	1-12, 13-24	Colossians	1-4
1 Kings	1-11, 12-22	1 Thessalonians	1-5
2 Kings	1-8, 9-17, 18-25	2 Thessalonians	1-3
1 Chronicles	1-9, 10-20, 21-29	1 Timothy	1-6
2 Chronicles	1-9, 10-24, 25-36	2 Timothy	1-4
Ezra	1-6, 7-10	Titus	1-3
Nehemiah	1-7, 8-13	Philemon	1
Esther	1-10	Hebrews	1-7, 8-13
Job	1-14, 15-21, 22-31, 32-42	James	1-5
		1 Peter	1-5
Psalms	1-41, 42-72, 73-89, 90-106, 107-150	2 Peter	1-3
		1 John	1-5
Proverbs	1-9, 10-24, 25-31	2 John	1
Ecclesiastes	1-12	3 John	1
Song of Solomon	1-8	Jude	1
Isaiah	1-12, 13-27, 28-39, 40-48, 49-57, 58-66	Revelation	1-5, 6-9, 10-18, 19-22
Jeremiah	1-10, 11-24, 25-33, 34-45, 46-52		
Lamentations	1-5		
Ezekiel	1-14, 15-24, 25-32, 33-39, 40-48		
Daniel	1-7, 8-12		
Hosea	1-8, 9-14		
Joel	1-3		
Amos	1-9		
Obadiah	1		
Jonah	1-4		
Micah	1-7		
Nahum	1-3		
Habakkuk	1-3		
Zephaniah	1-3		
Haggai	1-2		
Zechariah	1-8, 9-14		
Malachi	1-4		

saying in His Word and putting it down on paper keeps your mind out of neutral.

Even if you throw away your notes in a day or two, you will find they were worth the trouble. But you may want to keep them in a notebook or file. Using file folders labeled with the names of Bible books works well for this.

Keep It Simple

One pastor's wife I know often blows her husband a kiss during his sermons. Sounds romantic, doesn't it? But her kiss is to remind the Reverend of the acrostic *KISS*, which stands for "**K**eep **I**t **S**imple, **S**tupid!" That's also good advice for note-taking.

A good set of notes may be nothing more than the main points of a passage or a few general impressions from a chapter.

Another simple note-taking method involves underlining key words and phrases in the Bible. Some people even use a *color code* to represent certain basic Bible subjects, such as:

- *Red* for redemption
- *Blue* for heaven
- *Purple* for God the Father
- *Yellow* for the Holy Spirit
- *Orange* for Jesus
- *Brown* for judgment
- *Green* for what God wants me to do

You can use as many colors as you want, to stand for whatever topics you want to highlight. But do a little experimenting first to make sure your pens or pencils won't blur or soak through the pages of your Bible.

Symbols

Another fun way to take notes is to mark your Bible with *symbols*. Even simple punctuation marks written in the margin of your Bible will do the job:

? beside passages you have questions about (or questions God asks)

O beside significant statements

! beside commands God makes to us

" beside important quotes you want to recall

Or make up your own symbols. You don't have to be an artist. On page 39 are some sample ideas to get you started.

Using codes or symbols is an easy, fun way to take notes directly in your Bible. But sometimes you will probably want to go further in your note-taking.

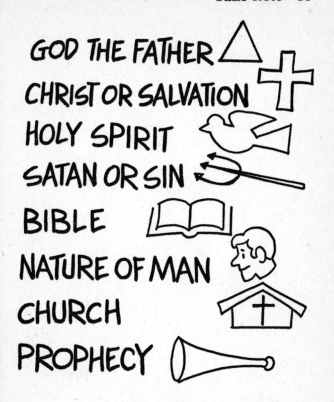

GOD THE FATHER

CHRIST OR SALVATION

HOLY SPIRIT

SATAN OR SIN

BIBLE

NATURE OF MAN

CHURCH

PROPHECY

What Are You Looking For?

"Aim at nothing and you will hit it every time." It's an old saying, but it's the plain truth about Bible study. So, before reading and taking notes on a Bible passage, decide what you want to look for in it. Rudyard Kipling's "six serving men" make good guidelines for what to look for as you read the Word:

I keep six honest serving men;
    (They taught me all I knew)
Their names are what and where and when
    And how and why and who.

Who? What? When? Where? Why? How? Some people like to take notes on all six questions at once. Others prefer to answer only one or two questions with each reading. Suit yourself! But try to keep at least one of these questions in mind each time you read.

Who? Who are the main characters in this book? Who is the author of this book, and what can I learn about him or her?

What? What is the main idea? What are the

major events? What are the key words?

When? When did the events take place? What can.I learn about the time period?

Where? Where did the action in this book take place?

Why? Why is this book or passage in the Bible? What would we be missing if we didn't have this Bible book?

How? How can I use the truths of this Bible book in my own life?

The rest of this chapter illustrates how using these six questions can make your Bible reading and note-taking more meaningful.

Who's Who?

Who are the main characters in this Bible book?
Take a few minutes right now to reread Jonah. As you read, list the major characters.

If you reread Jonah to find out who's who, you probably listed: (1) Jonah, (2) the sailors, (3) the ship captain, and (4) the people of Nineveh. You might also have listed Amittai, Jonah's dad. If you take a really broad view of the word "characters," you might also have listed "the Lord, the great fish, and the worm"!

In a short book like Jonah, it's OK to list all the minor characters. But in bigger books like Genesis, Joshua, Chronicles, or Luke, it's better to list just the major people.

Another *who* question you might ask is: **Who is the author of this book? What can I learn about him or her from reading this book?**

Thinking again of the Book of Jonah, Jonah himself may well have written the book that bears his name. The biggest clue is the first-person prayer in the second chapter.

What can you learn about Jonah from reading his book? He was a prophet. Jonah had a rebellious bent, but ended up doing God's will. He knew Scripture well, since he quoted a lot of it in chapter 2. Etc.

What's What?

To apply the question *what*, try to: **summarize the main idea of the book in one sentence.** For Jonah, a summary sentence might read, "Jonah tried to run from preaching in Nineveh, but he ended up there, and the city was saved."

Another way to apply the question *what* is to: **list all the major events of a Bible book in order.** Before you read further, try making a list of events in the Book of Jonah.

Here's what one young person wrote: "God called. Jonah ran. Storm arose. Sailors cast. Fish gulped. Jonah prayed. Fish spat. Jonah preached. Nineveh believed. God spared. Jonah cried. Worm chomped. God taught." You can be as simple or complex as you choose!

Another application of the *what* question is: **What are some key words in the book?** Here are some for Jonah: *Lord, fear, prayed.* There are others you might include. It is usually best to pick key words that are actually *in* the Bible passages (as opposed to words you make up *about* the text.)

Also, don't just pick out the words that are used the most, or you will end up with "key" words like: *the, and,* or *a.* Choose words that summarize important ideas, actions, or emotions.

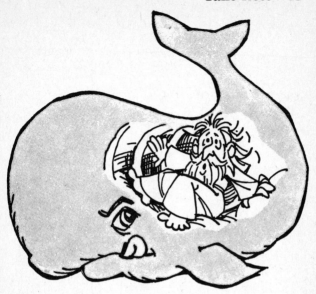

When Did It Happen?

When in history did the events in this book take place? What can I learn about the time period?

Just from reading Jonah, we know that the events had to take place when Nineveh was a great city. It was also a time when the Jews felt threatened by Nineveh's power.

Once you have noted these facts, you could look up the word Nineveh in a Bible dictionary or in any encyclopedia and find out that Nineveh was destroyed in 612 B.C. It would be safe to assume, then, that the events described in Jonah happened sometime before 612 B.C.! Look up the word Jonah in a Bible dictionary, and you will find more interesting facts about his life and times.

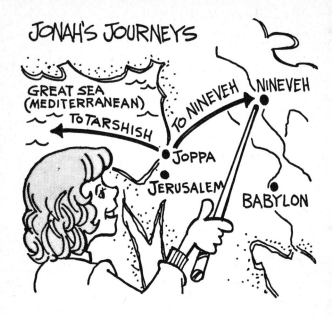

JONAH'S JOURNEYS

GREAT SEA
(MEDITERRANEAN)

TO TARSHISH

TO NINEVEH

NINEVEH

JOPPA

JERUSALEM

BABYLON

Where Were They?

Where did the action in this book take place?

For the Book of Jonah, general locations include: the sea, the ship, the shore, and the suburbs. Specific sites mentioned are: Nineveh, Joppa, and Tarshish.

What do you do when you read the names of ancient locations like these? Do you misapply the old Jewish principle of the Passover (that is, you *pass over* them)?

A better approach is to take a moment to look up such places on the maps in the back of your Bible. Or read about the locations in a Bible dictionary.

Why Keep This Around?

Why is this book in the Bible? What would we be missing if we didn't have this Bible book?

Jonah shows us how much God loved *all* the nations of the world, that He never loved just the Jews. Jonah also shows us how, as a loving Father, God disciplines His disobedient children so they will learn to walk in His ways.

Finally, what Jesus said in Matthew 12:38-41 (check it out) wouldn't make much sense if we didn't have the Book of Jonah.

How Can I Use It?

How can I use the truths of this book in my own life? How can this book help me be a better Christian this week?

One truth to apply from Jonah is that it's best to obey God the first time He calls us to do something. (But aren't you grateful for God's second and third chances?)

Another truth to apply is that God doesn't *force* us to obey Him, but He sure knows how to *encourage* us to obey. God didn't make Jonah go to Nineveh. But when Jonah was reluctant, God gave him three days and three nights of solitary confinement to reconsider his ways and come up with the right decision!

Body Building

Check out the sample form on page 47. You may want to use such a form for recording your answers to these six questions as you read a Bible book.

As you read and take notes, remember to start with the big picture (the main ideas of an entire book), then focus in on the individual parts. To say it another way, put together a skeleton, then put some meat on the bones.

Start today to use 1 or more of the techniques explained in this chapter to flesh out your understanding of one of God's 66 books.

My Personal Panorama of _____

W H O	Major People: _____ Author: _____
W H A T	Summary Sentence: _____ Major Events: _____
W H E N	Historical Setting: _____
W H E R E	Major Places: _____
W H Y	Why this book is in the Bible: _____
H O W	How this book can help me: _____

4

Choose Your Weapon

Did you ever try driving a car that was out of gas? Or going swimming in a desert? Or brushing your teeth without a toothbrush? Some things are just impossible to do without having one indispensable ingredient!

That's the way it is with Bible study. There is really only one "tool" that's absolutely necessary for reading and studying the Bible. And that's the Bible itself.

Which Version Is Best?

People often ask Karen and me, "Which Bible version do you recommend?" We do have an answer. But before we offer our opinion, check out the following quiz:

Which of the following three Bible versions seem the most understandable to you? (All three are versions of the same verse—Job 36:32-33.)
(1) "With clouds He covereth the light; and commandeth it not to shine by the cloud that

cometh betwixt. The noise thereof showeth concerning it, the cattle also concerning the vapor."

(2) "He fills His hands with lightning and commands it to strike its mark. His thunder announces the coming storm; even the cattle make known its approach."

(3) "He fills His hands with lightning bolts. He hurls each at its target. We feel His presence in the thunder. May all sinners be warned."

Did you choose number three? Most people do. "But it's not fair to pick an obscure reference from the Old Testament," someone objects. OK. Try one from the New Testament—2 Corinthians 6:11-13. Again, pick the version that seems the most understandable to you.

(1) "O ye Corinthians, our mouth is open unto you, our heart is enlarged, ye are not strai-

tened in us, but ye are straitened in your own bowels. Now for a recompence in the same, (I speak as unto my children,) be ye also enlarged."

(2) "We have spoken freely to you, Corinthians, and opened wide our hearts to you. We are not withholding our affection from you, but you are withholding yours from us. As a fair exchange—I speak as to my children—open wide your hearts also."

(3) "Oh, my dear Corinthian friends! I have told you all my feelings; I love you with all my heart. Any coldness still between us is not because of any lack of love on my part, but because your love is too small and does not reach out to me and draw me in. I am talking to you now as if you truly were my very own children. Open your hearts to us! Return our love."

You probably chose the third one again, didn't you? In both the New Testament and Old Testament examples, number one is from the *King James Version*. Number two is from the *New International Version*. And number three is from *The Living Bible*.

But before you jump to any conclusions about which Bible version is best, consider the scale on page 51. (Every Bible version could fit on this scale, ranked someplace between the most literal *translation* and the "loosest" *paraphrase*.)

What's the difference between the two? *Translations* bring every word of the original language (Hebrew and Aramaic for the Old Testament, Greek for the New Testament) over into English. The original word order may be changed to make sense in English. But every word from the original

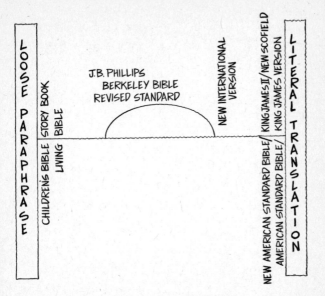

language is brought over into English.

Paraphrases, on the other hand, are only concerned with communicating the basic meaning of the original language. They don't bring every word from the original language into English.

A paraphrase is usually more readable than a translation. The language flows more smoothly, getting across the big ideas in everyday words. But the problem with a paraphrase is that it can be less accurate than a translation. The more someone summarizes the Bible's words into what he *thinks* the original author meant, the more room there is for error.

Translations are more accurate than paraphrases. But translations are also more formal, precise, and "text-bookish." As a result, they are harder to read and understand.

As the page 51 scale shows, some Bible versions are part paraphrase and part translation. They try to balance accuracy and readability.

Both Are Better

Which kind of Bible is better, translation or paraphrase? The answer is, both! It depends on your purpose.

Use a Bible version from the right side of the scale for detailed study, when *accuracy* is most important. Use a version on the left side of the scale for *overview reading,* to get the big picture.

If your goal is to read Leviticus or Luke in one sitting, you don't want a version that will make you scratch your head or dive for your dictionary every few lines. But don't depend on the easy-reading versions for serious Bible study. They're generally less accurate on the details.

To get the most out of God's Word, use at least two Bibles—one for the big picture and one for fine tuning on details.

Scaling the Versions

Look again at the scale on page 51. Notice how various Bible versions rank on the scale—from extremely literal on the right to extremely "loose" on the left. How much more accurate could you get than to read the Greek and Hebrew Bible manuscripts? (But even some scholars find them hard to read and understand!)

At the other extreme, what could be "looser"

than a children's Bible storybook? (By the way, reading a Bible storybook is a great way to get the big picture of the major people and events in the Bible. The only thing that might stand in the way is pride!)

On the page 51 scale, notice also that the *King James* (KJV) and *American Standard* (ASV) versions are the most literal versions we have in English. The *KJV* has been updated in more recent editions, such as *The New King James Bible* and *The New Scofield Reference Bible*. In these newer *King James* versions, words that have changed greatly over the nearly 400 years since the *KJV* was produced have been modernized. For example, "conversation" has been changed to "behavior"; "prevent" has been changed to "precede"; "suffer" to "allow."

The American Standard Version has also been modernized—in a new edition called the *New American Standard Bible* (NASB). The *KJV* and the *NASB* are widely used in Bible schools and seminaries because of their extreme accuracy.

The Living Bible is one of the all-time bestselling paraphrases. Ken Taylor began to rewrite the Bible in his own words for his children. He got so many requests for copies that he decided to publish it.

The Center Cluster

It's no accident that so many Bible versions fall toward the middle of the literal/loose scale. These middle-of-the-scale versions try to strike a balance between accuracy and readability. Middle-of-the-scale versions include J. B. Phillips' *New Testament in Modern English; The New Berkeley Bible* (some-

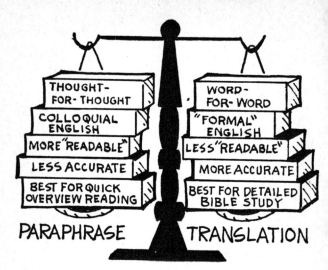

THOUGHT-FOR-THOUGHT
COLLOQUIAL ENGLISH
MORE "READABLE"
LESS ACCURATE
BEST FOR QUICK OVERVIEW READING
PARAPHRASE

WORD-FOR-WORD
"FORMAL" ENGLISH
LESS "READABLE"
MORE ACCURATE
BEST FOR DETAILED BIBLE STUDY
TRANSLATION

times called *The Modern Language Bible*); and the *New International Version*, one of the best of the newer versions. (Note where we rank it on the page 51 scale.)

There are many other versions to choose from. *The Amplified Bible*, for example, tries to give more of the many shades of meaning contained in the original language. Here's how John 3:16 reads in the *Amplified* version: "For God so greatly loved and dearly prized the world that He [even] gave up His only begotten Son, so that whoever believes in (trusts, clings to, relies on) Him may not perish—come to destruction, be lost—but have eternal (everlasting) life."

The *Good News Bible* (GNB) is a literal version with a simplified vocabulary. Originally designed for people using English as a second language, it has also sold well to people raised on English. (You might be more familiar with the New Testament portion of the *GNB* called *Good News for Modern Man*.)

The Study Bible

When choosing a Bible, also consider getting a good *study Bible*. Study Bibles have introductory pages to each of the 66 Bible books, summarizing at least the five "big Ws" (who, what, when, where, and why).

On every page are helpful cross-references and notes of explanation or interpretation. Many study editions use a "chain" approach, leading the reader from one passage to another in a progressive summary of Bible doctrines or teachings about the Christian life. At the front or back of all study Bibles are pages of outlines, charts, maps, and other useful information.

Here are some of the study Bibles Karen and I recommend. In parentheses we have noted which Bible version each study Bible uses.

- *The Thompson Chain Reference Bible* (KJV)
- *The Open Bible* (KJV or NASB)
- *The Ryrie Study Bible* (KJV or NASB)
- *The New Scofield Reference Bible* (updated KJV)

Cross-references Are All WET!

One of the least-used features of many Bibles is the *cross-reference*. Cross-references are those little verse numbers usually listed in the left- or right-hand margins of a Bible. Some Bibles have them in a center column. Cross-references are a guide to other Scriptures that shed light on the passage you are reading.

To remember how to use cross-references, just keep in mind that they are "all *WET*." A cross-reference gives new light on a:

Word (the same word used in another context);

Event (the same event discussed in another context); or

Thought (the same idea from another perspective).

Practice a moment on a verse in Jonah. Jonah 1:1 says, "The word of the Lord came to Jonah son of Amittai." Almost every Bible gives the following cross-reference for this first verse of Jonah: 2 Kings 14:25—"He was the one who restored the boundaries of Israel from Lebo Hamath to the Sea of the Arabah, in accordance with the word of the Lord, the God of Israel, spoken through His servant Jonah son of Amittai, the prophet from Gath Hepher."

Remember, cross-references shed new light on a **W**ord, **E**vent, or **T**hought repeated in both passages. For example, what new information about Jonah do you learn from 2 Kings 14:25?

We're told in this verse that Jonah was a prophet in his country of Israel. His hometown was Gath Hepher, wherever that is. (If you're curious, consult your Bible dictionary.)

We also learn from Kings that someone did something that Jonah had predicted would happen. In the verses just before 2 Kings 14:25, we discover that this someone was Jeroboam (also known as Jeroboam II), a king of Israel. That means that Jonah lived during or prior to Jeroboam's reign. A single cross-reference provides all this new information about Jonah.

NOTE: Sometimes a cross-reference listed with the first verse of a Bible book or chapter is meant to go with the *whole* book or chapter. The first verse just makes a convenient place to store the reference. (Read Jonah 1:1, then Matthew 12:39-41 for an example of this common technique.)

Making notes on what you learn from cross-references is a good method of Bible reading and study. Use the sample form on page 58, if you wish, to make cross-reference note-taking easier. (Try Genesis 10:11 on for size as a cross-reference to Jonah 1:2.)

The Bottom Line

Let's summarize.

(1) Every Bible version fits on a scale ranked someplace between the most literal *translation* and the "loosest" *paraphrase*. Which is better? Both are. A translation is best for detailed study, where accuracy is important. A paraphrase is best for overview reading, to get the big picture.

(2) A *study Bible* includes lots of extra information about what's recorded in God's Word. It combines the Bible text with Bible helps—both under one cover.

(3) Many Bibles contain *cross-references* in the margins of each page. Cross-references shed light on Scripture by comparing one verse to another.

It's important for a Christian to have a Bible version that works for the kind of reading and studying he does. It's great to have a good study Bible. But the most important things about a Christian and his Bible are that he reads it, believes it, and obeys it.

God's Commentary on _____

Cross-reference	SAME Word — Event — Thought	New information from cross-reference	How it affects me

5

Getting Organized

The subject was note-taking: "What do you do with the notes you take while reading and studying the Bible?"

Joe shrugged. "I don't do anything with them, 'cause I don't take notes. It's hard enough just finding time to read the Bible."

It was an honest answer. But Joe should be aware that taking notes could help him get more from his time in the Word. Here's how note-taking helps:

● Note-taking increases concentration and helps keep the mind from wandering.

● Note-taking helps a reader see how the parts of a Bible book fit together. (Since most people read and study the Bible a little at a time, it's sometimes difficult to see how all the smaller parts make up the big picture.)

● Note-taking helps a person *remember* more of what he reads and studies. He has to mentally distill the important ideas. Then he has to rethink those ideas while he writes them down. And he remembers more as a result.

Becky spoke up next. "I take notes. But I usually

throw them away later, or else they just get lost."

Taking notes on scraps of paper, then throwing them away—it may sound like a useless thing to do. Actually, Becky probably gets more out of her Bible study time than Joe does, simply because she does take notes. But she would benefit even more if she had a convenient way to organize and store the results of her note-taking efforts.

"I keep my notes!" Larry broke in. "They're right here." He thrust forward a well-worn Bible, bulging with old church bulletins, scraps of paper, and napkins with Bible verses scribbled on them. The binding of Larry's Bible seemed to groan under the strain of all the extra stuffing. And Larry had to admit that if he ever dropped his Bible, he'd lose his entire filing system!

A Personal Notebook

Though it takes a little extra time, it pays to get organized for Bible study, so we can keep the treasures we find in God's Word. A *personal notebook* can be a great help in organizing and collecting the results of Bible study and devotions.

Get a good quality vinyl or leather notebook, the kind you can add paper to. (You will want your personal notebook to be capable of lasting a long time, under heavy use.) Also get some tab dividers and label them according to the following subject areas:

(1) Personal Bible Studies. In this section, keep any notes you take during your personal Bible study time. Your notes might include chapter titles, outlines, charts, or any of the various Bible study *forms* explained throughout this book (such as the forms on pages 67 and 70).

(2) Prayer Requests. Write down specific prayer requests and record the date when you made each request. Leave space to come back later and record how God answered your prayer. (Check out the sample form on page 62.)

Keeping an up-to-date record of prayer requests and answers can be a super faith builder! As the pages grow, they become strong reminders that God is alive and well—that He does hear your prayers, and answers in His time and way.

(3) Sermon Notes. Use this section for storing notes you take on sermons and Bible messages. Try using a form like the one on page 63 for taking these notes.

PRAYER REQUESTS

"Praying always:... in the Spirit." (Eph. 6:18)

date	Request	date	answer

Sermon Notes

Subject: Date:
Scripture:
Speaker:
Main Idea:
Main points of Outline:

Development of Sermon or Lesson

Personal Application:

(4) Group Bible Studies. (You could use the same forms for this section as for your sermon notes.)

(5) Miscellaneous. Use this section for special handouts, church bulletins, quotations that are meaningful to you, illustrations you appreciate, or notes on Christian books other than the Bible. This section could even be used to hold lists of things you need to do, goals for the year or week, or almost any other information you need to keep up with.

A personal notebook can become an ongoing record of the things God is teaching you. It's a way to let the Lord know that you are paying attention to what He says to you, directly and through others. (See Hebrews 2:1 and Proverbs 6:20-21.)

Pile It or File It?

If you get involved in building a personal notebook, you will face a new problem sooner or later. Your notebook will fill up!

One solution is to get another notebook and start over. That's what Karen and I used to do. But once we had several notebooks sitting on a shelf, we decided there must be a better way. And there is—it's called "building a *personal file.*"

A filing system for Bible study material is easy to set up. And you don't need a fancy filing cabinet. All you need is a cardboard box large enough to hold a stack of letter-size file folders.

Buy a box of 100 letter-size folders. (The kind of file folders with reinforced tops are best because they last longest.) Use 66 folders for the 66 books of the Bible. Label each of the folders and organize

them according to the order the books appear in the Bible. Also prepare three folders labeled, "General Bible," "General Old Testament," and "General New Testament." The remaining 31 folders can be labeled with whatever topics you want to collect information about (for example, "The Church," "Witnessing," "Evidences for the Christian Faith," etc.)

As you file material, put general information about a Bible book in the front of the folder. File information about particular verses or chapters in order behind this general material. To make it easier to find the information you file, write the subject ("God Calls Jonah," etc.) or Bible reference ("Ephesians 2") in the upper right-hand corner of any papers you file.

A word of caution: Personal notebooks and files, once started, tend to collect a lot of material. Like growing gardens, they need occasional weeding!

Charting Your Course

One of the best ways of gathering material for a personal notebook or file is to chart your notes on a *Bible survey chart.* Look carefully at the page 67 sample chart on the Book of Ephesians. With paper, pencil, and a ruler, you can make your own blank charts for Bible study. (And relax. This Ephesians chart wasn't done in a single devotional period.)

Notice that the Ephesians chart is based on six "chapter titles." (Chapter titling is discussed in chapter 2 of this book.) The chapter titles are the "hooks" on which to hang other insights about the Bible book being charted.

Also notice that each vertical column on the chart represents one chapter of Ephesians. For smaller books (like Philemon, Jude, etc.) you could use one column per *paragraph.* For longer Bible books, study and chart them in segments. (Turn to page 36 to review some suggested subdivisions of larger Bible books.)

Genesis, for example, could be charted in four segments. You would chart Genesis 1—11 about the four great events: (1) Creation, (2) man's fall into sin, (3) the Flood, and (4) the tower of Babel. Your second chart on Genesis would include Genesis 12—25, which tells Abraham's life story. Other charts would cover Genesis 26—36 and 37—50.

Survey Chart: Ephesians

Chapter Titles	1 Chosen ones in Christ	2 Holy temple through grace	3 Revelation of one body	4 Intended growth to maturity	5 Spiritual walk at home	6 Total armor of God
TOPIC 1 Father	Chose us in Christ	Quickened us together with Christ	Revealed mystery of one body	Above all, through all, in all	To be followed; sends wrath on children of disobedience	Provides whole armor against devil
TOPIC 2 Son	Redeemed us through His blood	Reconciled Jew and Gentile to God	Gives access boldly to Father	Heads edifying of His body in love	Gave Himself for us in love	To be served as rewarder of men
TOPIC 3 Holy Spirit	Sealed us as purchased possessions	Lives in church as holy temple	Strengthens our inner man	Provides unity to body; seals us	Fills us to produce spiritual fruit	Gives sword, which is Word of God
Application 1	Let my life reflect God's glory	Treat my body as the Spirit's holy temple	Allow God to answer Paul's prayer for me	Grow in Christ today through His Word	Be thankful, even in hard times	Put on God's armor against Satan
Application 2	Pray for other believers like Paul did for me	Do the good works God planned for me	Do not limit God's power by my mind	Discover and develop my spiritual gifts	Let the Holy Spirit control me	Honor my parents
Insights	First ½ of book very doctrinal / last ½ very practical. Strong desire by author that truths of his writing grip and change readers. Many commands.					
Beginning and Ending	What to believe / how to behave. Spirit / Satan. Jew / Gentile. Old life / new life in Christ. What I am by nature / what I am in Christ.					

Topics, Anyone?

After writing chapter titles across the top line of a Bible survey chart, what goes in the rest of the boxes? Note on the far left side of the sample chart (page 67) where it says "Topics." To fill in these boxes, you would think of some subjects that pop up several times throughout the Bible book. These topics aren't necessarily in every chapter, but they are scattered throughout much of the book.

For example, for the Book of Jonah, what major topics come to mind? Well, there are a lot of miracles in Jonah, right? So you could label one topic line of your chart "Miracles." Then skim each chapter and list any miracles that are mentioned. Here's an example of what might be entered across your "miracle" line under each chapter of Jonah:

Chapter 1: God's Word came to Jonah; storm on the sea; lot fell on Jonah; sailors' conversion; great fish ready and waiting.

Chapter 2: Jonah remains alive and conscious; fish delivers him on dry land.

Chapter 3: Pagan Nineveh converted to God; God's judgment spared.

Chapter 4: Gourd; wind; worm.

If the Lord speaks to you, as you study, about something in your own life, jot it down on one of the "Application" lines under the appropriate chapter. What lessons for your life come to mind as you think about the miracles in the Book of Jonah? For example, under chapter 1 you might have noted the personal application, "God can turn my bunglings into great blessings."

The space labeled "Miscellaneous insights" is for any ideas you get that don't fit neatly in the other spaces. We don't want to limit the Lord just to what neatly fits into a box on a chart!

One such miscellaneous insight from Jonah might be: "God will use whatever miracles are necessary to encourage my obedience to His will. God loves His children so much that He won't let them get away with disobedience."

Or another general insight might be: "Nature seems to obey God faster than some believers!"

Some other major topics in Jonah which you might chart include: Jonah's attitude, God's mercies, repentance, people, and God's disciplines.

Suit Yourself

Choose the topics you want to chart on the basis of your own interests and findings. If you need help coming up with topics for a Bible book, ask yourself the following questions as you read: (You will remember them from chapter 3.)

What are some of the big ideas in this Bible book? What is the major activity? What is the mood?

Who are the main characters?

When are these things happening?

Where is the action taking place?

Why are these people doing what they are doing?

Answering these questions will lead you to discoveries about the Bible book which you can easily record on your chart for future reference.

Beginning and Ending

Another way to look at a Bible book is to compare its beginning and ending. In other words, ask

Survey Chart: Jonah

Chapter Titles	1 Jonah runs from God	2 Jonah repents inside fish	3 Jonah preaches in Nineveh	4 Jonah sulks outside city
TOPIC 1 Miracles	God's Word / storm / lots / conversions / fish	Jonah conscious / repents / delivered	Nineveh converted / judgment spared	vine / wind / worm
TOPIC 2 Prayer	Sailors to pagan gods / repent / to true God / vows	Jonah thankful to be alive, promises to obey	Ninevites repent / want compassion	Jonah asks God for death
TOPIC 3 Jonah's Attitude	Disobedient & fearful	Distressed & remorseful	Denouncing evil	Discouraged
Application 1	God can turn my bunglings into blessings!	God strongly *encourages* my obedience!	Past mistakes don't have to hold me back!	God patiently deals with my bad attitudes!
Application 2	My sins affect others!	It's the Bible in my heart that counts!	I should never give up hope for anyone.	Ask questions when counseling someone.
Insights	God loves His children too much to let them get away. Nature seems to obey God faster than some believers. God loves everyone in the world.			
Beginning and Ending	Jonah in Israel / Jonah in Nineveh. Nineveh destined for destruction / God spares Nineveh. Sailors worship pagan gods / sailors worship true God. Jonah runs from Nineveh / Jonah goes to Nineveh.			

"How have things changed during the course of this book?" (Notice that there is a place on the charts on pages 67 and 70 to record these findings too.)

For example, how is the last chapter of Jonah different from the first one? For one thing, Jonah's location has changed. In chapter 1 he's in Israel, but in chapter 4 he's in (or at least near) Nineveh. Another change is that Nineveh is destined for destruction when the book opens, but by the close of Jonah, God has spared the city. Before reading on in this chapter, see how many more contrasts between the beginning and ending of Jonah you can find.

Some other contrasts you might have noted are:

● Sailors worship pagan gods/sailors worship true God. (The contrasts don't have to happen just in the first and last chapters. The idea is to note any changes that happen during the course of the book.)

● Jonah runs away from Nineveh/Jonah goes to Nineveh.

● Jonah is disobedient to God/Jonah obeys God.

You will be surprised at how much you can learn about a Bible book just by thinking through the changes that happen between its beginning and ending.

In Closing

Remember that it takes time and a lot of study to complete a Bible survey chart like the ones on pages 67 and 70. Don't get discouraged if you don't have all the boxes filled after one day.

And don't lose sight of the ultimate goal of per-

sonal notebooks, personal files, and Bible survey
charts. The ultimate goal is *spiritual growth*. We
should always be asking ourselves as we study:
"What new truth have I learned about God? About
myself? About what God wants me to do?"

God didn't give us His Word just so we could fill
in spaces on a chart or in a notebook. But personal
notebooks, files, and Bible survey charts can help
us understand God's Word, organize and store the
treasures we find there—*and* put into practice what
we learn.

6

Zooming In

Studying the Bible is like examining a specimen under a microscope. We can study a big chunk of the Bible, paying little attention to the smaller details, or we can zoom in on the smaller parts for a close-up look.

The preceding chapter of this book, chapter 5, explained how to study Bible *books*. This chapter, chapter 6, tells how to zoom in on Bible *chapters and*

paragraphs. The next chapter, chapter 7, tells how to focus in on *sentences and words* in the Bible.

Comprehending Chapters and Probing Paragraphs

As a rule, if a Bible book has three chapters or less, dig into the *paragraphs* as your basic study units. But study longer books *chapter by chapter*.

(NOTE: In some Bible versions, it's difficult to know where paragraphs begin and end. If you need help picking out the paragraph divisions in your Bible, check out Appendix A in the back of this book.)

What should you look for in a Bible chapter or

paragraph? Take your pick of any or all of the following categories. (Keep your Bible open to the first chapter of Jonah as we learn how to get more out of Bible chapters and paragraphs.)

1. Chapter or paragraph titles. Start by making your own chapter or paragraph titles, as described in chapter 2 of this book. Try to limit each title to four words or less.

2. Characters. Ask, "Who are the main characters in this section?" For Jonah 1, you might list the following characters:

- the Lord
- Jonah
- the captain
- the sailors
- the great fish

3. Places. Ask, "Where is the action taking place?" In Jonah 1, action sites include:

- Nineveh
- Joppa
- Tarshish
- the sea
- the ship
- in the great fish

(NOTE: Not every Bible chapter or paragraph mentions people or places.)

4. Ideas or events. Some Bible chapters and paragraphs consist mainly of events—people *doing* something. Other sections are mainly ideas—thoughts on a subject. Job, Psalms, Proverbs, and the New Testament letters (Romans through Jude) consist mainly of ideas. The other Bible books consist mainly of events.

When focusing on the ideas or events in a chapter or paragraph, making a *summary list* is a good idea. For example, Jonah 1 consists mainly of events. They might be summarized as follows:

- God calls Jonah to preach in Nineveh.
- Jonah gets on a boat going the wrong way.
- God sends a great storm on the sea.
- The sailors throw Jonah overboard.
- A great fish picks up Jonah.

5. Mood. Ask, "What is the dominant mood of the main character(s) or of the author?"

The dominant mood in Jonah 1 is *fear*. Jonah was afraid to go to Nineveh. The sailors were afraid in the storm. Jonah claimed that he feared the Lord. The sailors developed a proper fear of God through their experience with Jonah.

6. Summary verse. Ask, "If I were to pick one verse out of this section to sum it all up, which verse would I choose?"

For Jonah 1, verse 3 is a good summary verse: "But Jonah ran away from the Lord and headed for Tarshish. He went down to Joppa, where he found a ship bound for that port. After paying the fare, he went aboard and sailed for Tarshish to flee from the Lord."

7. Summary words. Ask, "If I were to pick one or two words out of this section to sum it all up, which would I choose?"

For Jonah 1, a good summary word is "fleeing" (v. 3). Though it is only used once in the entire chapter, it describes Jonah's main activity. Other summary words for Jonah 1 might be "ship" or "storm."

8. Similarities. Ask, "What similarities between various parts of this section can I find?"

Similarities might include words or phrases which are repeated, or ideas and events which are similar in some way. For example, here are some similarities found in Jonah 1:

● The word "great" is repeated a lot: Nineveh was a great city (v. 2). God sent a great wind (v. 4), causing a great storm (v. 12). The ship's crew greatly feared the Lord (v. 16). God provided a great fish for Jonah (v. 17).

● Also in Jonah 1, the storm is mentioned repeatedly. And it grows in intensity through verses 4, 11, 12, and 13.

● There are several "miracles" in this chapter: God sends the great wind and storm (v. 4). He causes the lot to fall on Jonah (v. 7). God calms the sea (v. 15). He prepares the great fish for Jonah (v. 17).

9. Contrast. Ask, "What contrasts can I find when I compare people, events, or ideas in this section?" Here are some contrasts found in Jonah 1:

● God told Jonah to go to Nineveh (v. 2), but Jonah ran in the opposite direction (v. 3).

● While the crew was fighting the storm on deck, Jonah was sound asleep below deck (v. 6).

● The crew started out as pagans (v. 6), and ended up as believers in God (v. 16).

● The sea was stormy with Jonah on board (vv. 4-14), but calm with Jonah overboard (v. 15).

10. Principles to live by. Ask, "What important lessons does the Bible teach in this chapter or paragraph?" A "principle to live by" is like the "moral of the story."

Here are some principles to live by, found in Jonah 1: (See how many others you can come up with.)

● God uses *people* to do His work (v. 1).
● God calls specific people for specific tasks (vv. 1-2).
● God warns people of judgment before He sends it (v. 2).
● Favorable circumstances alone are not always a reliable indicator of God's will (v. 3).
● God sometimes disciplines His children when they disobey Him (v. 4).
● Our sins affect others around us (v. 4).

Most of the principles to live by that are found in Jonah 1 are not directly stated. They are only *implied*. For example, most people would agree that Jonah 1 teaches the above principle: "Our sins affect others around us." But what verse in Jonah 1 specifically states those words? Not a single verse! But even though this principle is not directly stated, it is strongly implied.

It's perfectly OK to discover implied principles in a Bible chapter or paragraph. But it also can be dangerous. The danger is that we could read something into God's Word that's not there.

To guard against this possibility, God has given a safeguard: "Every matter must be established by the testimony of two or three witnesses" (2 Corinthians 13:1). When we think we see an implied principle, we can check ourselves by looking for the same idea in two or three other Bible passages. If we can find two or three other places in the Bible where the same principle is clearly taught, then we are on safe footing.

But how do we find those other passages? Checking out the *cross-references* printed in many

Bibles is a good place to start. Another good place to look is in a *topical Bible*, which groups Bible verses according to subject.

Here's another key word to keep in mind when looking for implied principles in the Bible: *context*. Check out the diagram on page 81, and remember: to study a Bible word, sentence, paragraph, chapter, or book, always read at least the next larger circle. To study a word, at least read the sentence in which it is found. Before tackling a sentence, at least read the paragraph that includes it—and so on.

One way that cults get started is by people spreading false teaching based on Bible verses that have been yanked out of their contexts!

11. Questions. As you study a Bible chapter or paragraph, note any questions that you have.

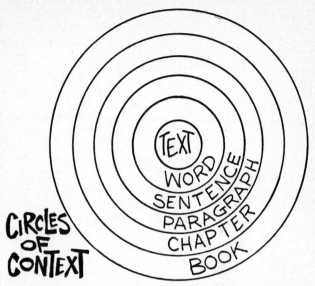

CIRCLES OF CONTEXT

Even if you don't answer all your questions right away, jotting them down will give you something to think about. And maybe you will want to search out the answers at some point.

When you are ready to track down some answers, how do you do it? Cross-references in your Bible can help. So can a *Bible dictionary* or a *Bible encyclopedia*. For the tough questions, you may need to check a *Bible commentary*. (Chapters 7 and 8 of this book describe some tools that are helpful in answering questions about Bible passages.)

And don't overlook the value of a regular set of encyclopedias. For example, read about whales in an encyclopedia and you will find out that some whales would have had no trouble swallowing Jonah whole. Sperm whales have been found with gullets measuring 10 feet!

My Chapter or Paragraph Study in _____

Chapter Title: _____
Paragraph Title(s): _____

Characters: _____

Place: _____

Ideas or Events: _____

Mood: _____

Summary Word(s): _____

Summary Verse: _____

Similarities: _____

Contrasts: _____

Principles to Live by: _____

Questions to Answer: _____

Miscellaneous Insights: _____

What I Plan to Do: _____

12. Miscellaneous insights. This category is a catch-all for anything you see in a chapter or paragraph that doesn't fit into one of the other 11 categories.

Form Your Own Conclusions

On page 82 is a sample form you can use with any of the techniques described in this chapter for analyzing a Bible chapter or paragraph. Treat this form like a smorgasbord table. Pick and choose categories according to your own appetite and personal tastes. You don't *have* to use the whole form. And you don't have to complete it in one or two sittings. More important than getting through a lot of the Bible is letting part of the Bible get through to you—and make a difference in your life.

13. "What I plan to do". Give special attention to this last item on the sample form. Learning a lot of Bible facts without applying them to our lives can be deadly, in a spiritual sense.

Growth in Bible knowledge should never be confused with growth into Christlikeness. It's important to jot down something specific that we plan to *do* as a result of studying a chapter or paragraph of God's Word.

7

The Word Finder

Justin zipped his warm-up jacket, pulled his Bible out of his gym bag, and sat down. The cool grass under the shade of an elm tree felt refreshing.

Suddenly a pistol shot cracked. But Justin ignored it, as he did the other sights and sounds of the track meet. Already he had run in the 880-yard race, the first of his three scheduled events. And now coach Hennesey had asked him to fill in for Brent Crawford in the two-mile relay. This meet would call for something extra from Justin, and he knew it. So he had slipped away after the 880 for a few minutes of rest and quiet with the Lord.

He flipped through Psalms and read a few verses as they caught his eye. But none seemed to speak to him. He prayed, asking the Lord for strength to do his best in the rest of his events.

Then a thought rustled through Justin's mind: *strength . . . like an eagle.* That was all—just those four words.

"What is that verse?" he wondered out loud. "Something about an eagle flying. . . ." He opened his Bible and flipped through the pages again, then closed it. "It's no use. I'll never find that verse without knowing the reference."

He prayed some more, then pulled himself up and jogged back down the hill toward the track. He felt better, and he knew God was with him. But somehow Justin felt the Lord had a special message for him. If only he could have found it.

Actually, Justin could have found it—easily. The *concordance* in the back of Justin's Bible would have led him straight to the verse he wanted to locate.

Here's how. First, using just the four words that he could remember, "strength . . . like an eagle," Justin could have picked one *key word* to look up in the concordance. (In Justin's case, the word "eagle" would have been a good one to look up.) Looking up the word "eagle" in his Bible concordance, here's what he would have found:

E

eagle, *bird of falcon family*

Dt 32:11   As an e. stirreth up
Ps 103:5   renewed like the e.
Is 40:31   with wings as e.
Jer 4:13   horses swifter than e.
Mt 24:28   there will the e. be

(Notice that the word under consideration, "eagle," is abbreviated.) A concordance also shows some of the words that surround the main word in the Bible. So Justin could have picked out the verse he had in mind without looking up all the references to "eagle." After finding the "address" (the verse number) for his verse, Justin could have turned right to it in his Bible where he would have read: "They that wait upon the Lord shall renew their strength; they shall mount up with wings as eagles; they shall run, and not be weary; and they shall walk, and not faint" (Isaiah 40:31, KJV).

The Right "Address"

Next to the Bible itself, two types of books are probably the most important Bible study tools available. One is a *Bible dictionary*, discussed in chapter 8. The other is a *Bible concordance*.

A lot of Bibles contain the kind of concordance found in the back of Justin's Bible. This type of concordance is known as a partial, or *abridged*, concordance because it contains a limited number of the words found in the Bible. The main use of an abridged concordance is for finding a Bible passage when you don't know its "address," as in the example of Justin and his "eagle verse."

Another kind of concordance comes in its own separate volume, because it is too big to be combined with the Bible. This kind of concordance lists almost every word in the Bible and every place where each word occurs.

These concordances are called complete concordances or *exhaustive* concordances. (They are called "exhaustive" because of their thoroughness, not because they tire out their users!)

The least expensive, and probably the most widely used, complete concordance is *Cruden's* concordance. But at least three other complete concordances are even more helpful than *Cruden's*. They are (1) *Strong's*, (2) *Young's*, and (3) *The New American Standard* exhaustive concordances.

In addition to containing nearly every word in the Bible, these three concordances also tell what every word means in the original language (Hebrew or Greek). And you don't need to know any Hebrew or Greek to use them.

The only differences between these three concordances is that they are organized a bit differently or they use different Bible versions. (*Strong's* and *Young's* use the *King James* version. The *New American Standard* concordance uses the *New American Standard Bible*.)

Cutting through the Versions

"Who cares what Bible words meant in the original languages?" someone asks. "It all sounds pretty *exhausting to me!"*

Here's why the "original-language" feature of an exhaustive concordance is important:

We have many accurate, reliable versions of the Bible in English. But all of them are at least one step removed from the original words. (They have been translated from Hebrew and Greek.) An exhaustive concordance offers a way to "cut through" all the versions and get back to the original word meanings.

An exhaustive concordance with original-language definitions can solve a common two-sided problem: (1) The same Greek or Hebrew word gets translated into two or more different English words, and (2) two or more different Greek or Hebrew words get translated into a single English word.

An example of the same Greek word getting translated into more than one English word can be seen in the familiar "love" passage in 1 Corinthians 13:

> Charity never faileth: but whether there be prophecies, they shall fail; whether there be tongues, they shall cease; whether there be knowledge, it shall vanish away. . . . But when that which is perfect is come, then that which is in part shall be done away. When I was a child, I spake as a child, I understood as a child, I thought as a child; but when I became a man, I put away childish things. (1 Corinthians 13:8, 10-11, KJV)

In these verses, the phrases "shall fail," "shall vanish away," " shall be done away," and "put away" all come from a *single* Greek word.

English Bible versions also provide many examples of different Greek and Hebrew words getting translated into a single English word. For instance, the original words *sheol*, *hades*, *gehenna*, and *tartarus* are all translated into one word, "hell," in English Bibles. And two Greek words, *agapé* and *philéo*, are both translated into the same English word—"love."

John 21 illustrates the importance of being able to trace an English word back to its original Greek meaning. In this passage, Jesus asks Peter three times, "Do you love Me?" The first two times, the Greek word *agapé* is used. But the third time, the word *philéo* is used. *Philéo* is different from *agapé* in that it more clearly expresses the idea of a "tender affection."

John 21:15-17

¹⁵When they had finished eating, Jesus said to Simon Peter, "Simon son of John, do you truly *agapé* me more than these?"

"Yes, Lord," he said, "you know that I love you."

Jesus said, "Feed my lambs."

¹⁶ Again Jesus said, "Simon son of John, do you truly *agapé* me?"

He answered, "Yes, Lord, you know that I love you."

Jesus said, "Take care of my sheep."

¹⁷The third time he said to him, "Simon son of John, do you *philéo* me?"

Peter was hurt because Jesus asked him the third time, "Do you love me?" He said, "Lord, you know all things; you know that I love you."

Jesus said, "Feed my sheep."

If we just read an English version of this passage, we would miss this subtle change, because

"Blessed"

Job 29:11 the ear heard me, then it *b* me: 833
    31:20 If his loins have not *b* me. and if   1288
    42:12 So the Lord *b* the latter end of   ..
Ps   1:1 *B* is the man that walketh not   835
    2:12 *B* are all they that put their   ..
  18:46 Lord liveth; and *b* be my rock;   1288
    21:6 hast made him most *b* for ever: 1293
    28:6 *B* be the Lord, because he hath   1288
    31:21 *B* be the Lord: for he hath   ..
    32:1 *B* is he whose transgression is   835
      2 *B* is the man unto whom the Lord   ..
  33:12 *B* is the nation whose God is the   ..
  34:8 *b* is the man that trusteth in him.   ..
  37:22 For such as be *b* of him shall   1288
    26 and lendeth; and his seed is *b*.   1293
  40:4 *b* is that man that maketh the   835
  41:1 *B* is he that considereth the poor: ..
    2 and he shall be *b* upon the earth: •833
  41:13 *B* be the Lord God of Israel   1288
  45:2 therefore God hath *b* thee for ever.   ..
  49:18 while he lived he *b* his soul: and   ..
  65:4 *B* is the man whom thou choosest,   835
  66:20 *B* be God, which hath not turned   1288
  68:19 *B* be the Lord, who daily loadeth   ..
    35 power unto his people. *B* be God.   ..
  72:17 sun: and men shall be *b* in him: ..
    17 him: all nations shall call him *b*.   •833
    18 *B* be the Lord God, the God of   1288
    19 *b* be his glorious name for ever: ..
  84:4 *B* are they that dwell in thy house: 835
    5 *B* is the man whose strength is in   ..
    12 *b* is the man that trusteth in thee.   ..
  89:15 *B* is the people that know the   ..
    52 *B* be the Lord for evermore.   1288
  94:12 *B* is the man whom thou   835
 106:3 *B* are they that keep judgment,   ..
    48 *B* be the Lord God of Israel from   1288
 112:1 *B* is the man that feareth the Lord,   835
    2 of the upright shall be *b*.   1288
 113:2 *B* be the name of the Lord from   ..
 115:15 Ye are *b* of the Lord which made   ..
 118:26 *B* be he that cometh in the name   ..
    26 we have *b* you out of the house of   ..
 119:1 *B* are the undefiled in the way,   835
    2 *B* are they that keep his   ..
    12 *B* art thou, O Lord: teach me   1288
 124:6 *B* be the Lord, who hath not   ..
 128:1 *B* is every one that feareth   835
    4 thus shall the man be *b* that   1288
 135:21 *B* be the Lord out of Zion, which   ..
 144:1 *B* be the Lord my strength,   •
 147:13 he hath *b* thy children within   ..
Pr 5:18 Let thy fountain be *b*: and rejoice   ..
  8:32 for *b* are they that keep my ways.   835

90

the single word "love" is used for both *agapé* and *philéo*. Fortunately, with the help of an exhaustive concordance, we can check out the original word meanings for ourselves.

How to Do It

Tracking down word meanings in Greek and Hebrew may sound difficult. It's not. But you will need to try out a few words for yourself, instead of just reading about how to do it. Work through the following exercise for a step-by-step lesson. (You won't need a concordance for this exercise.)

Bible words in a concordance are arranged alphabetically, just like in a dictionary. Remember, to look up a word in *Cruden's, Strong's, Young's,* or the *NAS* concordances, you have to start with a word from either the *King James* or *New American Standard* versions of the Bible.

Suppose you are reading your Bible one day and come across the word "blessed" in Psalm 119:1— "Blessed are the undefiled in the way, who walk in the Law of the Lord" (KJV). You decide to look up "blessed" in *Strong's Concordance*.

If you were really using the concordance, your first step would be to look for "blessed" in the alphabetically arranged list of words. But for now, just use the sample column from *Strong's* on page 90.

Having found your word ("blessed"), run your finger down the list of verses to the one you started with (Psalm 119:1). Notice that all the references are arranged in the order they appear in the Bible.

At the end of the partial quotation of the verse is a number—#835. This number is a simple key for finding the original Greek or Hebrew word. When there is not a number at the end of a line, that means the word was supplied for clarification by the Bible translators, and has no original word to support it.

The next step is to turn to the appropriate dictionary at the back of the concordance. Use the "Greek Dictionary" (the last section in *Strong's*) for New Testament references. Use the "Hebrew and Chaldee Dictionary" (the next-to-the-last section in *Strong's*) for Old Testament references.

Looking up #835 in the Hebrew Dictionary, here's what you would find:

835. אֶשֶׁר 'esher, *eh´-sher;* from 833; *happiness;*
          only in masc. plur. constr. as interjec.,
how *happy!:*—blessed, happy.

The italicized English words are the definitions. So now you know that "blessed," as used in Psalm 119:1, comes from the Hebrew word *esher* meaning "happiness" or "how happy!"

Now insert the definitions in place of your original word ("blessed"). Use any of the italicized definitions which make sense in your verse. Psalm 119:1 then reads: [*How happy*] are the undefiled in the way, who walk in the Law of the Lord" (KJV).

The words listed after the sign, :—, are all the English words in the *King James* Bible which were translated from the Hebrew word *esher*. In this case, there are only two: "blessed" and "happy."

This is as far as you would usually go in tracking down a word in a concordance. But for super-serious Bible students, the following activity can yield even deeper insights into God's Word.

For the Super-serious Only

Sometimes a definition in the Hebrew or Greek dictionary section refers the reader to a "root word." For example, look again at the definition of *esher* on page 92. Notice the words, "from 833." This number is a reference to the *primitive root* of the word translated "happiness" in Psalm 119:1. Turning to #833, here is what you would find:

833. אָשַׁר 'âshar, *aw-shar'*; or אָשֵׁר 'âshêr, *aw-share'*; a prim. root; to *be straight* (used in the widest sense, espec. to *be level, right, happy*); fig. to *go forward, be honest, prosper:* (call, be) bless (-ed, happy), go, guide, lead, relieve.

Applying the italicized definitions to Psalm 119:1, we find that the word translated "blessed" comes from a root word meaning to be *straight, right, happy, going forward, honest,* and *prospering!*

The Bible translators couldn't include all of these "root" definitions in the English version of Psalm 119:1. So they used an English word that seemed closest to the meaning of the original Hebrew word. But with a concordance, we can uncover some of the rich meaning of the original Hebrew word which may have been lost in translation.

Caution: The definitions that we have uncovered for "blessed" as it is used in Psalm 119:1 may not apply to the word "blessed" as used in other verses. For example, look back at the column of verses under "blessed" (page 90).

● Is the same Hebrew word for "blessed" also used in Psalm 119:2? (Yes. We know that because it has the same number—#835.)

● Is the same Hebrew word for "blessed" used

in Psalm 119:12? (No. It has a different number—
#1288.)

If you were to look up #1288 in the Hebrew and
Chaldee dictionary section, you would find:

1288. בָּרַךְ **bârak,** *baw-rak´;* a prim. root; to
kneel; by impl. to *bless* God (as an act of
adoration), and (vice-versa) man (as a benefit); also
(by euphemism) to *curse* (God or the king, as trea-
son):—× abundantly, × altogether, × at all, blas-
pheme, bless, congratulate, curse, × greatly, ×
indeed, kneel (down), praise, salute, × still, thank.

What is the basic meaning of root word #1288?
(''To kneel or to bless God as an act of adoration.'')

Now look at the distinction you have uncovered
between Psalm 119:1 and 119:12—God blesses us
(v. 1) by making us happy, honest, prosperous,
etc. We bless Him (v. 12) by kneeling in adoration!

Expand Yourself

One of Karen's and my favorite Bible study methods is to make our own *expanded version* of a Bible
verse, using our *Strong's Concordance.* Here is an
example of how we would make an expanded
version of Proverbs 1:5. First, we look up the definitions of key words in the verse. The following
list shows *Strong's* numbers and partial definitions
for some of the key words in Proverbs 1:5.

**Definitions of Terms in Proverbs 1:5 from Strong's
Concordance:**
"Wise": (#2450) intelligent (knowledge), skillful (ability),
artful beauty, gracefulness)

"Hear": (#8085) Hear intelligently with implications of attention and obedience

"Increase": (#3254) Add, augment, continue to do a thing

"Learning": (#3948) Something received (From 3947—basic root meaning to "take away")

"Man": (No number means not in original: word supplied by translators)

"Attain": (#7069) Erect, create, procure by purchase, to own

"Counsels": (#8458) Good advice, guidance, steering (From #2254 and 2256: wind tightly, as a rope; bind by a pledge)

"Understanding": (#998) To separate mentally; distinguish; perceive

Proverbs 1:5 (KJV)
"A wise man will hear, and will increase learning; and a man of understanding shall attain unto wise counsels."

Next we rewrite the verse, inserting the definitions in parentheses.

Expanded translation using Strong's Concordance definitions:
A wise (intelligent, skillful, artful) person will hear intelligently (with implications of attention and obedience) and will increase (continue to augment) learning (what is received and taken away);

And a person of understanding (able to mentally separate and distinguish) shall attain (procure for his own possesion) wise (intelligent, skillful, artful) counsels (good advice guiding one as though bound by a pledge, like a rope being wound tightly).

There it is—Halls' expanded version of Proverbs 1:5!

Some people get scared off by the size of an exhaustive concordance such as *Strong's* or *Young's*. (They are big!) But learning to use one is not as hard as many people think. And the rewards are great.

That's why, if I could only have three books, one would be an exhaustive concordance. The other two would be a Bible and the special tool described in the next chapter.

8

The Gap Jumper

Science fiction writers have twisted the plot a thousand different ways, but it's still the same basic set-up— A modern-day earthling rockets into outer space and discovers a world that is literally light-years different from our own.

He crawls out of his spaceship and peers up at the sky, hoping to figure out some basic directions. But instead of fastening on our familiar yellow sun, his eyes squint at five flourescent-green cubes on a hazy purple horizon.

Eventually, the moment of truth comes as Earthling meets up with the planet's inhabitants. If he is lucky, they don't zap him into galactic oblivion. But even if he survives, he's got some *major* problems to deal with.

He says hello. And the friendly space creatures answer back with voices that sound like synthesized chipmunk chatter.

Earthling uses sign language to let them know he is hungry. So they politely haul out their favorite food, poached meteorites, and stuff it in his ear.

To further complicate his predicament, Earthling figures out that his ship has broken through some edge-of-space time warp. If he is ever able to get back to earth, he sadly realizes, the year will be A.D. 4583.

We rarely think of the Bible world as an "alien" environment. But if we were able to travel back in time to the world of Moses and Abraham, we would be almost as lost as Earthling in outer space. The Bible has come to us from an ancient, "alien" world. And the fact is, we need to understand that world in order to accurately understand the Bible. A *Bible dictionary* can help provide that understanding.

A good Bible dictionary is like a mini-encyclopedia. It supplies information on all the *people* (2,930 people mentioned in the Bible), *places* (1,551 places referred to in Scripture), and on most of the other difficult *words* of the Bible.

A Bible dictionary is important because of the following "gaps" that sometimes make the Bible hard to understand:

Time gaps. The most "recent" events described in the Bible happened about 1,900 years ago. Parts of the Bible were written by Moses over 3,400 years ago. And some of the events which Moses wrote about happened thousands of years before that.

Language gaps. The Bible was originally written in Greek, Hebrew, and Aramaic. The best known English translation, the *King James Version*, was produced over 350 years ago.

Culture Gaps. The setting of the Bible is an ancient Oriental culture. Its customs often seem unfamiliar, even bizarre, to 20th-century Bible readers.

Geography gaps. The events of the Bible took place in the Middle East, in places most modern readers have never heard of, much less seen.

A Bible dictionary can bridge these gaps between the world of the Bible and our modern world.

Checking for Gaps

How many of the following 20 words from the Bible can you identify or define?

1. habergeon
2. Chislev
3. Artaxerxes
4. Shushan
5. concision
6. lasciviousness
7. concupiscence
8. reprobate
9. Nisan
10. tetrarch
11. Elul
12. Abib (not the kind a baby wears)
13. Zif
14. Tammuz
15. Sivan
16. Tebeth
17. Bul
18. Ethanim
19. Adar
20. Shebat (not a female bat!)

(HINT: Half of the words in the above list have something in common. Of the 20 words listed, 10 are Jewish names for months of the year.)

How did you do? (If you knew 15 or more of those words, you're ready to teach in a Bible college. If you knew 10-14, get ready to graduate *magna cum laude maximus* from Sunday School. If you only knew 0-6, you're normal!) For the correct answers, consult a Bible dictionary.

It's not the kind of book you would want to curl up with for an evening of light entertainment. But as you come across unfamiliar words or ideas in the Bible, a quick check in a Bible dictionary can make your understanding mushroom.

For an example of how a Bible dictionary can fill

in the gaps in your understanding of the Bible, read through the Book of Jonah again. (It's only four chapters, remember?) As you read, jot down any words that represent "gaps" for you (for example, "Jonah," "Nineveh," "Tarshish," "lot"). Then look up each word in a Bible dictionary before reading any further in this chapter.

Depending on which Bible dictionary you read, you will have discovered many of the following insights about the size and power of Nineveh:

Nineveh and its suburbs stretched across 30 square miles. It would have taken the average Ninevite about 3 days to walk from one end of the metropolis to the other.

The central city was surrounded by 8 miles of high walls (40-50 feet tall), plus a moat formed by the Tigris River. Nineveh's walls were topped by a hundred lookout towers. These walls were 50 feet thick, so thick that the Ninevites grew crops on top of them and could drive 3 chariots, side by side, across the tops of the walls.

There were probably 600,000 people living in the central city of Nineveh in Jonah's day. This is the proud, self-secure city God brought to its knees with a few words from the foreign prophet, Jonah!

Looking up Nineveh (the city) or Assyria (the country) would also give you some idea of the Ninevites' reputation for cruelty:

Asshurbanipal, one of the Assyrian rulers, was known for cutting off the hands and lips of his victims. King Tiglath-pileser would flay conquered enemies alive (peel off their skin), then stack their skulls in a huge pile. Other Assyrian rulers would cut off the feet of the people they conquered. As the capital of Assyria, Nineveh was the center of a ruthless world power, a country the rest of the world hated and feared.

Getting a handle on some of this background information brings new insight into the Book of Jonah. For example, knowing about Nineveh's reputation for cruelty helps explain why a prophet of God (Jonah) would be tempted to run away from God's call. Prophesying against Nineveh would be like walking up to the Incredible Hulk and tweaking his nose!

All in a Name

Taking the time to look up the *names* of people and places in a Bible dictionary pays off in other ways. For one, a Bible dictionary shows how to pronounce unfamiliar names correctly. With the help

of a Bible dictionary, you will be able to slip your tongue smoothly over names like Artaxerxes, Nebuchadnezzar, Mahalaleel, Arphaxad, Nebaioth, or Zerubbabel. And a Bible dictionary can give you a feel for the land of the Bible, putting you at ease with places like Adramyttium, Abel-beth-maachah, Almon-Diblathaim, Aruboth, Ataroth, and Azmaveth.

Also, Bible names are frequently crammed with meaning. And often a person's name has significance concerning his character or life work. For example, "Abram" means "exalted father." God changed his name to "Abraham," meaning "father of multitudes." His wife's name was changed from "Sarai," meaning "contentious," to "Sarah," meaning "princess."

Even those long *lists* of names that appear throughout the Bible can come alive when you understand what the names mean.

Expanding Your Tool Collection

This chapter and the preceding one have dealt with the two most important Bible study tools (next to the Bible itself)—the concordance and the Bible dictionary. But other helpful tools are available, including a:

● **Bible handbook**—a mini-commentary which summarizes and explains each of the 66 books of the Bible;

● **Bible atlas**—maps, photographs, and historical information about places in the Bible;

● **Bible commentary**—gives interpretations of Bible passages.

See Appendix B at the back of this book for some specific recommendations regarding these and other Bible study helps.

If we honestly believe that *all* Scripture is "God-breathed and useful" (2 Timothy 3:16), we will treat every *word* in God's Word as necessary and important.

Right now, why not pick out a Bible passage and look up the key words in whatever tools you have available at the moment (even if nothing more than a regular English dictionary as a starter)? Begin to experience some of the wonder built into the world of Bible words!

9

Mostly for Fun

Looking up "root words," taking notes, using a Bible dictionary. . . . Even if you recognize the value of Bible study, it can sometimes seem too much like schoolwork!

When the idea of getting into God's Word sounds about as enjoyable as doing homework on a Saturday night, try one of the activities described in this chapter. It just might add the creative touch you need to put some fun back in your Bible study.

Good News

One way to have fun with God's Word is to play the part of a newspaper editor living and working during Bible days. What you "publish" looks somewhat like a modern-day newspaper, except everything in it is based on a part of the Bible. For example, the items in *The Genesis Times* (pages 106-107) were all created by young people using stories and ideas found in the Book of Genesis.

Here are some of the features you could include in your own Bible newspaper:

THE GENESIS TIMES

NEWS
EDITORIALS
WEATHER
GAMES
PERSONALITIES
WANT ADS
ADVERTISEMENTS

ARK COMPLETED

Noah has completed construction of his ark. Its measurements are 450' x 75' x 45'. It is made of gopher wood and covered with tar. It has a door on the side and one window, near the top. Inside there are three decks divided into numerous rooms.

The ridicule and criticism of Noah continues. Nothing of this magnitude has ever been constructed before this time. Noah continues to claim that God instructed him to build this ark. When asked why God wants this ark built, Noah replied that God will destroy all life on the earth by means of a great flood. Only those on the ark will be saved. This report has failed to create any local interest in obtaining passage on the vessel.

Noah is reported to have decided to bring aboard his ark seven pairs of some animals and one pair of other animals. The only human beings interested in this ark are those in Noah's family. At the time of this article, provisions of food and water were being placed aboard the ark. (Gen. 6:5--7:4).

ANNIVERSARY OF FIRST MURDER

Tomorrow will mark the anniversary of the world's first murder case. The following is a copy of the original article covering the trial that followed.
CASE NO. 4:1-15
****

The blood of the first murdered man entered the ground today. The man was Abel, the son of Adam. The killer was his older brother, Cain.

The trial that followed was very dramatic. The judge was God and there was no jury. Cain chose to defend himself. The prosecuting attorney was the voice of Abel's blood crying to the Judge from the ground.

The background of the murder is this:

Cain was a farmer and he used his "fruits of the ground" as an offering to God. Abel, on the other hand was a shepherd, and he gave his best stock to the Lord. God accepted Abel's

106

FIRST MURDER
(CONTINUED)

offering; but not Cain's.

Because of this, Cain was very angry. Sometime later, when both were in the fields, Cain killed Abel.

When the Judge asked Cain if he knew where Abel was, Cain replied, "I do not know. Am I my brother's keeper?"

Then came the voice of the prosecuting attorney, and it was all over for Cain's lies.

The verdict was reached, Guilty! His sentence was this:
1. His crops would never grow.
2. He would be a vagabond and a wanderer on the earth.

Then Cain said to the Judge, "My punishment is too great to bear!" The Judge put a mark on Cain and said that if anyone kills him, that person will receive seven times the punishment.

ANNOUCEMENTS

MARRIAGES:
On the sixth day of Creation, Adam married Eve in the Garden of Eden. Those attending included the birds and beasts of the earth. The ceremony was performed by the Lord God. (Gen. 1:27; 2:18-25)

BIRTHS:
Adam and Eve announced after leaving the Garden of Eden, the birth of their first and second sons, Cain and Abel. (Gen. 4:1-2)

FOR SALE: Two slightly useless fig leaves. (Gen. 3:7)

- Masthead at top of first page
- Headline and lead news story
- Other news stories
- Editorials
- Want ads
- Advertisements
- "Photos" (drawings, stick figures, etc.)
- Letters to the editor
- Cartoons
- Crossword puzzles
- Interviews
- Fashions, Domestics, Recipes
- Sports, Travel, Business
- Short "human-interest" items

You don't have to "publish" your newspaper alone either. Just about anything goes better when you do it with someone else, and making Bible newspapers is no exception. Several people can work together, each writing a different part of the paper. Let an "editor" put the parts together, use a photocopy machine for your printing press, and you've got it!

With a group or by yourself, try your hand right now at creating one or two newspaper features based on the Book of Jonah. Start with something simple, like a *want ad*. For example, an employment want ad might read: "Prophet wanted. Must be willing to follow orders. Position requires transfer to Nineveh."

Writing little *news tidbits* is also an easy place to start. A page titled "Nineveh Notes" could have entries such as the following: "As revival continues, religious services have been instituted in the palace ballroom." Or "Governor returns 5 million stolen rubles to the province coffers."

Or try writing a *women's page feature* using the

following headline: "New Fall Fashions from Nineveh—Sackcloth for a Simpler Lifestyle."

It might sound morbid, but writing an *obituary* is a fun way to review your knowledge of Bible characters. It gives the opportunity to summarize the character's major accomplishments and the lessons to be learned from his or her life. Try writing the obituary of a lesser known Bible person, such as Jonah's father Amittai, or the King of Nineveh.

Or try putting together an *interview* with any of the characters in Jonah, perhaps the captain of the ship. You're not limited to interviewing people, either. Retell the events of the Book of Jonah through the eyes of "the great fish." Ask, "What was it like to have to stomach a disobedient prophet? Did it cause indigestion?" Etc.

Let your creative juices flow! Enjoy retelling part of the Bible in a newspaper format.

Something Old, Something New

Did you ever wish you could write songs? Here's your chance at musical stardom—and you don't have to know anything about music. All you need to do is make up new words to fit an old tune.

Just take a familiar tune and count the number of syllables per line. For example, the first line of "Jesus Loves Me" has seven syllables: "Jesus loves me, this I know." The second line also has seven. The next step is to make up some new lines with the same number of syllables as the original tune.

Here's a song some young people composed, using the tune of "Jesus Loves Me" to tell the story of Jonah and the whale:

Jonah went against God's wish;
So he wound up in a fish!
Nineveh turned to the Lord;
But the worm got that old gourd!
    (chorus)
Don't be like Jonah!
Don't be like Jonah!
Don't be like Jonah!
Accept God's perfect will!

Game Time

One of the easiest ways to add some fun to Bible study is to make a biblical game out of a "secular" one. Many common games such as Parcheesi or Monopoly can be transformed into Bible games just by coming up with your own Scripture questions.

One easy-to-make Bible game combines a Parcheesi board with a deck of homemade Bible question cards. In order to move forward on the board, a player has to correctly answer a question card. When a player misses, he has to look up and read aloud the correct answer from the Bible.

The other players will try to remember the answer because the question card is shuffled back into the deck and some lucky player will get the same question again later in the game. Each question card might also contain instructions similar to the following: "If you answered correctly, move forward three spaces," or "If you answered incorrectly, return to START."

Question What You Read

You can spice up your daily Bible reading, and build a deck of question cards, by making up your own game questions as you read. And they don't have to be just Bible *facts*. They can also be questions that help players *apply* God's Word to their lives. Here are some examples of practical-minded questions from the Book of Proverbs:

(1) Why is it wrong to be completely "open-minded"?

(2) What kind of a fool should be avoided?

(3) How can you recognize a prostitute?

(4) How can you recognize a lazy person?

(5) Why is it foolish to hope in "get-rich-quick" schemes?

(6) What can other people learn about you by observing the type of friends you pick?

(7) Why should you never rejoice when your enemy falls?

(8) What's the only thing worse than being a fool?

(Answers to the above are found in the Book of Proverbs.)

You can be as humorous as you want in making up Bible questions. For some "biblical" chuckles, check out the following examples:

(1) Who was the shortest man in the Bible?

(2) Who was the tiniest man in the Bible?

(3) Who was the straightest man in the Bible?

(4) When was tennis played by two Bible characters?

(5) What time of day was Adam created?

(6) What did Adam and Eve do after God expelled them from Eden?

(7) When was a rooster's crow heard by every living creature on earth?

(8) Who was the most successful doctor in the Bible?

(9) Who was the first Irishman mentioned in Scripture?

(See answers to the above in Appendix C.)

Crosswords

Another mostly-for-fun activity is to create your own crossword puzzle in which all the words come from a section of the Bible. The crossword puzzle on page 113, for example, is based on the Book of Jonah. (You can find the answers in Appendix D.)

It's not hard to make your own Bible crossword puzzle. Simply read a section of the Bible, making a list of key words (important people, places, and events). Then begin to interlace these words on a

JONAH CROSSWORD

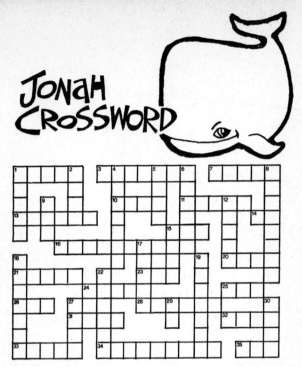

Puzzle clues are based on the NEW INTERNATIONAL VERSION of the Bible. The location of words on the puzzle, and the Bible verses which contain the words, are given in parentheses. For example, (30-D, 1:1) indicates that number 30-Down may be found in Jonah 1:1. (Puzzle answers are given in Appendix D.)

The (30-D, 1:1) of the (15-D,1:1) came to (1-A, 1:1) telling him to go to (3-A, 1:2). But Jonah (25-A, 1:3) to (1-D, 1:3) to board a ship bound for (8-D, 1:3) and (26-A, 1:5) down. Then the Lord sent a (19-D, 1:4) (33-A, 1:4) on the sea. The (18-D, 1:7) said, "Let (14-A, 1:7) cast (20-A, 1:7)," and they (21-A, 1:8) Jonah questions. Jonah claimed to worship the (35-A, 1:9) of (6-D, 1:9). He said, "Throw (29-D, 1:12) (32-A, 1:12) the sea. (4-D, 1:13), the sailors rowed harder. Finally they threw Jonah (31-A, 1:15) and made (5-D, 1:16). But a (7-A, 1:17) fish swallowed Jonah, who (13-A, 2:1) to his (23-A, 2:1). Though he felt banished from God's (17-D, 2:4), engulfed by the (22-D, 2:5), and barred in by the (24-A, 2:6), Jonah looked toward God's (28-A, 2:7). When the king of Nineveh heard God's warning, he took off his (12-D, 3:6) robes and put on (34-A, 3:8). God had (16-A, 3:10) and spared the city. Jonah became (11-A, 4:1) because God was (10-A, 4:2) to anger. So Jonah (9-D, 4:5) watching the city until a (27-D, 4:7) ate his shade plant. God asked Jonah, "Do you (2-D, 4:9) a right to be angry?"

113

piece of paper in crossword fashion. (Some people use the letter tiles of a "Scrabble" game to form their puzzle layout.) After getting in all the big words you can, read your Bible section again and fill in your puzzle with some short "filler" words.

Tell It Your Way

Chapter 4 discussed a kind of Bible version called a *paraphrase*—a retelling of Bible truths in simpler, more modern language. One more way to have some fun with Bible study is to make up your own Bible "paraphrase." Here's how John Duckworth retold Jonah's tale in modern form:

"Joan and the Whale"

Joan was in her dorm room eating an *Oh Henry* bar, listening to the radio, and having her quiet time, all at once. Suddenly, the Lord spoke to her. Out of respect, she stopped chewing and turned the radio down a little.

"Joan," said God, "I want you to arise and go across the hall to Min Niniver, a girl who lives in Room 207. And I want you to be her friend."

Joan giggled. Her laughter made her fish-shaped earrings and her cross necklace shake. "C'mon, God," she said, " don't kid me. I'm a busy person. You know perfectly well I've got to study hard so I can go and be a missionary for You over in Upper Tarshishstan." She giggled again.

But God indicated He was very serious. He did not sound very amused.

Joan closed her Bibles (several versions) and

frowned at the ceiling. "Lord," she said, "that's simply out of the question. Min Niniver's the girl they call 'the Whale.' She must weigh 250 pounds. If I were seen with her, I'd be a social outcast." She tossed her candy wrapper in the garbage. "And that would just *ruin* my witness!"

There was silence. Joan looked up at the ceiling again, but only saw the light fixture. To her surprise, God did not speak again.

In fact, she didn't hear a word from Him—not even a postcard—for the next six months. Not that she worried about it too much. She was very busy these days, and before she knew it Joan was ready to fly away to Upper Tarshishstan.

So she packed her suitcase full of missionary stuff and boarded a plane to the faraway land. But the Lord sent along three skyjackers on her flight, and halfway across the Atlantic Ocean they pulled out their guns and hand grenades. And everyone was sore afraid.

Everyone, that is, except Joan. She was sound asleep in her seat, next to a nervous hardware salesman from Trenton, N.J.

"Wake up!" cried the salesman, shaking Joan. "How can you sleep through this? We're being skyjacked!"

Joan opened her eyes. "What?" she mumbled.

"I notice you wear a cross," the salesman said frantically. "Maybe if you pray—"

Joan brightened. "I'm glad you made that suggestion," she said, whipping out her New Testament. "Let me witness to you." She proceeded to read 34 verses to the hardware salesman, as well as to a lady senator, two Army generals, a baseball player, and several ministers.

Suddenly one of the skyjackers burst into the

cabin. "Awright," he yelled, "I want one hostage. We're going to let the rest of you go."

The passengers cheered and pointed at Joan. "Take *her!*" they shouted in unison. A sigh of relief echoed up and down the aisles as she was led away.

Soon the plane landed, and the passengers were set free. But Joan was tied up in the cargo hold. And she was in the belly of the plane for three days and three nights.

Then Joan prayed to the Lord from the belly of the plane, saying, "OK, God. I get the picture. If You get me out of here, I'll go back and witness to the Whale . . . I mean, to Min."

And God said, "Who said anything about witnessing? I just said to be her 'friend.'"

"Gotcha."

And the Lord spoke to the skyjackers, and they threw Joan out on the landing strip.

So Joan returned to her dorm room. And in a few months she was Min Niniver's friend. It took a lot of work, but lo and behold—after almost a year—Joan introduced Min to her Friend, God. And the three of them became better friends than ever.

Finally one day the Word of the Lord came to Joan a second time, saying, "Joan, arise—"

"Oh, no," said Joan. "Where to this time?"

"Why, to Upper Tarshishstan, of course," said God.

"Ahhh," said Joan.

This time she took a boat.

10

Stopping the
Great
Brain Drain

How's your thought life? Would you like for more of your thoughts to be in tune with God's thoughts? Would you like to come to the place where, more and more, you "automatically" do God's will? The key may be a process which the Bible calls "the renewing of your mind" (Romans 12:2). Here's why.

Our minds are like icebergs. Only the smallest part of an iceberg is visible above the water line. The largest part floats hidden beneath the surface. The conscious part of our minds is only a small part. The subconscious part is much larger. Though hidden "below the surface," the subconscious mind controls much of what we think, feel, and do.

In the computer room of a Chicago bank is a large sign that reads, "Garbage in—Garbage out!" It's a reminder that the data coming *out* of a computer can't be any more accurate than what is fed *in*.

"Garbage in—garbage out" also applies to the

mind. Everything we have ever taken in through our five senses has been recorded in the vast computer network of our subconscious minds. Much of our behavior is controlled "automatically" from our subconscious. For example, driving a car often becomes a subconscious activity. We've done it so many times that it becomes "automatic." We don't have to think about what to do next, we just do it.

Do you see why God places such importance on "renewing the mind"? Our minds need to be continually cleansed and renewed. And the only effective "brain cleanser" is God's Word!

As we take in God's Word, it is stored in the subconscious mind. As we get the Word in us, it goes to work, cleaning up the "garbage" inside (Hebrews 4:12). Ultimately, God's Word—stored in the subconscious mind—begins to influence how we think, how we feel, and how we act!

For our own good, then, God has commanded us to memorize and meditate on Scripture. (See Deuteronomy 6:4-6 and 11:18; Joshua 1:8; Proverbs 7:1-3; and Colossians 3:16.) And He has promised a number of benefits that can be ours as a result of storing His Word in our minds and hearts. Some of these benefits include:

- victory over sin (Psalm 119:9-11);
- answers to prayer (John 15:7);
- spiritual growth (Psalm 1:2-3);
- wisdom and skill in living (Psalm 119:97-100);
- inner joy (Jeremiah 15:16); and
- mental transformation (Romans 12:1-2).

Memorizing Scripture is obviously important. But how do we do it? Let's use the word *REMEMBER* as an acrostic reminder of eight ways to memorize God's Word faster and easier:

Reach for a definite goal.

Expect God's help.

Make cards for review.

Emphasize the meaning of the passage.

Meditate on the passage.

Beware of mental garbage.

Enlist the help of a friend.

Review! Review! Review!

Reach for a Definite Goal

Decide how much you want to memorize and how long you plan to take. Then break your goal into "bite-sized" steps. For example, to memorize 10 verses about salvation in 10 weeks, learn at least one verse per week. To memorize the entire Book of Philippians in a year, you only need to learn two verses a week.

A friend challenged Karen and me to memorize the Book of James. We didn't think we had the mental machinery to remember a whole book of the Bible. But our friend pointed out that, since James only has 108 verses, we would only have to memorize 2 verses a week to learn the whole book in about a year.

So we accepted the challenge. Two verses a week—that we could handle. And by breaking the project into bite-sized chunks, we reached our goal. In a year's time, we memorized the Book of James.

We also found that while we were working on James, it was working on us. The more we memorized, the more we felt like Mr. James had been reading our minds. God's Word was cleaning out the "garbage"!

Goals for Bible memorization will differ from person to person, of course. Ask the Lord to show you how much Scripture He wants you to memorize. If you need some suggestions on where to start, check out Appendix E in the back of this book.

Expect God's Help

Jesus said, "When He, the Spirit of truth, comes, He will guide you into all truth. . . . He will bring glory to Me by taking from what is mine and making it known to you" (John 16:12, 14). One of the reasons God sends the Holy Spirit to live in all of His children is to help us learn and understand the Scriptures.

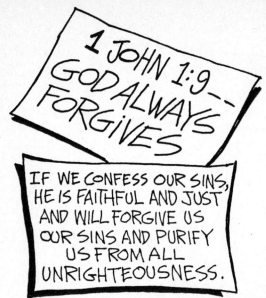

Let's face it. Memorizing Scripture takes some self-discipline. But don't depend on your own strength. Pray for and expect God's help as you allow His Spirit to work in you.

Make Cards for Review

Try writing out memory verses on small cards to carry with you. Then review the verses during spare moments of waiting, walking, shaving, and other routine activities when you would normally coast in mental neutral.

Write out the Scripture portion on one side of the card with its reference and/or topic idea on the other side (for example, 1 John 1:9—GOD AL-

WAYS FORGIVES). Then you can review from both directions. Taping Scripture verse cards to mirrors and other often-looked-at places also works well for review.

There's an important benefit of *writing out* your Scripture verses for review: Copying the verses helps in memorization.

Long before Israel had its first king, God gave some rules for future kings to follow (Deuteronomy 17:14-20). One of these rules said that the first thing a new king should do is "write for himself" a personal copy of God's Law (v. 18). "God's Law" would have included at least the whole Book of Deuteronomy, if not all of the first five books of the Bible!

Why make such a rule? The Lord knew that copying Scripture is a better way to learn it than just reading it. Besides, how could a king claim ignorance of the Law as an excuse for breaking it if he had personally copied it all?

Right now pick out a verse and see how quickly you can learn it by copying it from your Bible onto a piece of paper. Then try writing the verse from memory. When you have written all of it you can recall, correct your paper, filling in any missing parts. Continue this process till you have the verse memorized. Karen and I find that it usually takes only about six or seven copyings till we can write a verse from memory.

Emphasize the Meaning of the Passage

Don't be guilty of memorizing words without knowing what they mean. You'll get as much out of that kind of memorization as the little boy who drew the following picture after hearing about God "driving" Adam and Eve out of the Garden of Eden:

Another illustration of learning words without understanding their meaning is the child's picture, on page 124, of Pontius "the pilot" taking Joseph and Mary on the "flight to Egypt".

To avoid this problem, look carefully at each key word in your memory verse and ask yourself what it means. Then look up any words you can't define. Use a regular dictionary, a Bible dictionary, or a concordance.

Make sure you read some of the verses surrounding the one you plan to memorize. This will also help you better understand your memory verse.

Try reciting your memory verse out loud, giving special emphasis to each key word. For example: "*I* can do everything through Him who gives me strength. I *can* do everything through Him who

gives me strength. I can *do* everything through Him who gives me strength. I can do *everything* through Him who gives me strength."

Reciting Scripture this way, out loud, not only emphasizes key words and their meanings, it also helps you remember. The following percentages represent how much we remember after three days, using six different methods of learning:

- Reading—10%
- Hearing—20%
- Seeing—30%
- Seeing and hearing—50%
- Studying—60%
- Saying out loud—70%!

Meditate on the Selected Scripture

Meditation involves thinking and praying about a particular Scripture till it becomes something more to you than just words in your head. One of the best ways to do this is by turning a Scripture passage into a first-person prayer to God. (This process is explained more fully in chapter 11.)

Any verse can become a prayer of thanks, help, or confession. For example, instead of just reciting Philippians 4:13, you could *pray* it something like this: "Thank You, Lord, that I can do everything through Christ who gives me strength. Please help me to do everything through Your strength and not my own."

Also, ask yourself how the Scripture passage applies to your life at the present time. Here are three questions that can help you get to the heart of what God wants to say to you from a particular passage:

(1) What does God want me to *know?*
(2) How does God want me to *feel?*
(3) What does God want me to *do?*

Beware of Mental Garbage

Remember how we got into this discussion of Scripture memorization? We suggested that memorization can play an important part in cleansing and renewing the mind of a Christian so he can overcome sin and grow spiritually. "I have hidden Your Word in my heart that I might not sin against You" (Psalm 119:11).

But although the Word can cleanse our minds, it's just as important that we guard against the intake of impure thoughts. "Finally, brothers, whatever is true, whatever is noble, whatever is right, whatever is pure, whatever is lovely, whatever is admirable—if anything is excellent or praiseworthy—think about such things" (Philippians 4:8). Those are instructions from the Manufacturer of our minds!

Our computer-like minds work on the principle of *association*. (This principle is at work when you link a new fact with an older, well-known fact in order to remember something for a test.) Our mind also stores associated material together. Every time we repeat an experience or expose ourselves repeatedly to the same material, it becomes that much more "built in" to the mind's storage system.

If, for example, a guy feeds lustful material into his mind by what he reads and looks at, he's manufacturing a time bomb. The detonation will come in a moment of temptation. But the temptation is like the wind felling a tree which has been

rotting for a long time.

No wonder that in a Bible chapter which deals with how a young person can avoid sin, Solomon advises, "Above all else, guard your heart, for it is the wellspring of life" (Proverbs 4:23). The word "heart" as used here and elsewhere in the Bible refers to the *mind*, emotions, and will.

We need to take in the Word so it can do its cleansing work in us. But we also need to shut out mental mind pollutants whenever we have the choice. We don't have to read or watch *everything* that's available to us. We don't have to listen to *every* conversation.

The forces of darkness are waging an all-out battle for control of our minds. The evangelist D. L. Moody described how the battle is won or lost: "Either this Book [the Bible] will keep you from sin, or sin will keep you from this Book."

Enlist the Help of a Friend

Solomon, the wisest man who ever lived, said: "Two are better than one, because they have a good return for their work: If one falls down, his friend can help him up. But pity the man who falls and has no one to help him up! Also, if two lie together, they will keep warm. But how can one keep warm alone? Though one may be over-powered, two can defend themselves. A cord of three strands is not quickly broken" (Ecclesiastes 4:9-12).

Almost everything works better when friends share the load. Memorizing Scripture is no exception. To memorize a passage faster and more easily, try practicing out loud with another person.

Then plan times of "checking up" on each other for review.

If you don't have a "spiritual partner" with whom you can share common memorization goals and encouragement, ask the Lord to send you one.

Review! Review! Review!

Memory is not Sanforized—it is subject to shrinkage! The cure is regular review. Do you ever get discouraged because you learn a verse one day and can't recall it at all the next day? Don't be! Karen and I find that it takes three or four weeks of re-learning a verse daily till it is really "at home" inside us.

Can you recite John 3:16? Say it to yourself right now. Have you reviewed this verse recently? Probably not. Yet you probably were able to recite it without looking it up in your Bible.

You probably learned John 3:16 a long time ago and have heard it often since then. Any part of God's Word can become a part of us, like John 3:16, if we give it the same attention and review. "Overlearning" a passage so that it comes to mind almost automatically only happens by constant repetition over a period of time. Once the passage has been thoroughly learned, less frequent review will keep it fresh in your mind.

Getting Started

How's your thought life? No matter what condition it's in now, memorizing Scripture can transform it—and turn your life around.

Don't be overwhelmed if storing the Word in your mind seems "too much" for you. Could you sit down right now and eat 100 pounds of hamburger? Hopefully not! But you'll probably take in more than that amount over the next year, and most of it a bit at a time! It's amazing how much spiritual food we can eat in a year's time by taking a "bite at a time."

So pick a Scripture passage—and a friend—and get started!

Reach for a definite goal.
Expect God's help.
Make cards for review.
Emphasize the meaning of the passage.
Meditate on the selected Scripture.
Beware of mental garbage.
Enlist the help of a friend.
Review! Review! Review!

11

A New Set of
SPECS?

"It is not enough to own a Bible; we must read it. It is not enough to read it; we must let it speak to us. It is not enough to let it speak to us; we must believe it. It is not enough to believe it, we must live it."

—William A. Ward

When our involvement with God's Word only goes as far as reading, studying, and memorizing it, spiritual indigestion can result. The next two steps, *meditation* and *application,* make Bible study something more than just a mental exercise.

To make a difference in our lives, God's Word needs to work in three areas: the mind, the emotions, and the will. Reading, studying, and memorizing Scripture gets the Word into our minds; meditation gets it involved with our emotions; and application deals with our wills.

Meditation and application go hand in hand. You meditate on a Bible passage by thinking it over prayerfully till it speaks to you in a *personal* way. Then the logical outcome of meditation is deciding how God wants you to put your personal insights into practice—that's application.

Pray It Back

There are many ways to meditate on God's Word. One excellent way is to quote a Bible passage back to God in a first-person prayer.

For example, first read the following verses from the Book of James:

> James, a servant of God and of the Lord Jesus Christ, to the 12 tribes scattered among the nations: Greetings.
>
> Consider it pure joy, my brothers, whenever you face trials of many kinds, because you know that the testing of your faith develops perseverance. Perseverance must finish its work so that you may be mature and complete, not lacking anything. If any of you lacks wisdom, he should ask God, who gives generously to all without finding fault, and it will be given him. But when he asks, he must believe and not doubt, because he who doubts is like a wave of the sea, blown and tossed by the wind. That man should not think he will receive anything from the Lord; he is a double-minded man, unstable in all he does.
>
> (James 1:1-8)

Now compare the following first-person prayer to the above passage:

"Father, I thank You that James was Your servant as well as the servant of the Lord Jesus Christ. I also want to be known as one of Your servants. Please help me to bring Your Good News to other people.

"When I face trials of many kinds, help me to be joyful.' Help me to realize in such times that the testing of my faith is developing endurance. Please help me to grow in endurance and faith so I can become more like Jesus.

"Dear Father, when I lack wisdom, remind me to ask You for it. Thank You that You give generously to me without finding fault. Please help me to believe and not doubt when I ask You for help and wisdom with my problems and decisions. I don't want to be like a wave of the sea, blown and tossed by the wind. I want to receive what I ask from You. I don't want to be a double-minded person who is unstable in all I do.

"In the name of Jesus, Amen."

Notice how this kind of personalized prayer brings God's Word "close to home"? No longer is the passage just talking about some ancient apostle who wrote to somebody, somewhere, way back when. Praying back Scripture gets our emotions *personally involved* with what God is saying to us in His Word.

Before you read any further in this chapter, try turning a Bible passage into a personal prayer. Use a passage of your choice or continue with James 1, starting with verse 9.

A Self-check Quiz

Another way to meditate on a Bible section and get more personally involved with it is to give yourself a true-false quiz. Simply go through a Bible passage and ask yourself if what you are reading is true of you or not. For example, here are some sample questions based on the passage already quoted (James 1:1-8):

Am I a servant of the Lord?

Am I joyful when I face trials?

Do I believe that the testing of my faith develops endurance?

Am I becoming spiritually mature by trusting the Lord during trials?

When I lack wisdom, do I turn to God first?

Do I view God as someone who gives to me generously without finding fault?

When I ask God for wisdom, do I ask doubting or believing?

Am I double-minded and unstable in my ways?

As we ask ourselves these questions, we're visualizing how the passage fits our lives—and how our lives fit the passage. And the truth of God's

Word is moving from our minds into the sphere of our emotions and experience.

A New Set of SPECS?

Stuart didn't believe the state driver's license examiner. *There must be something wrong with his machine,* Stuart figured. *I can see OK.* But a second opinion proved Stuart wrong. He needed corrective lenses.

The most amazing surprise came when he put on his new specs for the first time. Everything looked so much clearer and sharper! Stuart hadn't realized what he had been missing.

SINS TO FORSAKE
PROMISES TO CLAIM
EXAMPLES TO FOLLOW
COMMANDS TO OBEY
STUMBLING BLOCKS TO AVOID
? "WHAT SHOULD I DO NOW?"

There's a set of specs available to help you see more in the Bible. The acrostic *SPECS?* stands for six things to look for as you meditate on a Bible passage and decide how to apply it to your life:

Sins to forsake
Promises to claim
Examples to follow
Commands to obey
Stumbling blocks to avoid
?"What should I do now?"

The idea is to read a Bible passage and make notes of what you learn in any of the six *SPECS?* categories. Once you get used to using your new *SPECS?* you can look for insights in all six categories during a single reading. Or you can re-read the same passage on separate days, looking for a different part of *SPECS?* each time.

Sins to Forsake

Try out the first letter of *SPECS?* with the first chapter of Jonah. Read Jonah 1 and note any sins which are to be forsaken.

Here are some insights you may have noted regarding specific sins:

(1) Disobedience to God's revealed will (vv. 1-3). Jonah knew he was supposed to be in a certain city with a certain message. He not only refused to go, but actually ran in the opposite direction!

(2) Trying to run from the presence of the Lord (vv. 2-3, 10).

(3) Not caring for the welfare of others (Nineveh, vv. 1-3; sailors, vv. 4-11).

(4) Not letting our "walk" match our "talk" (compare vv. 9 and 10).

Other "sins to forsake" could be found in this

chapter. But didn't you find you got more from the chapter because you were looking for something in particular as you read?

Promises to Claim

Now look for any promises to claim in Jonah 1.

Find any promises? You won't always find insights for each category in *SPECS?* But even when you don't, you will get more from a Bible passage by looking through your *SPECS?* than by just reading aimlessly.

Though you probably didn't find any *direct* promises to claim in Jonah 1, you might have written down something similar to the following: "No matter where I run, God is there." If so, what you have seen with your *SPECS?* is an *implied* truth. It's a truth that comes through clearly from the passage even though it's not directly stated.

Implied Bible truths can be just as valid as directly stated ones. But we should be cautious in drawing implications from a passage. The danger is that we might be reading something into the Bible which God never intended to say.

How do we stay on firm footing as we look for implied truths in Scripture? Remember that the guiding principle is, "Every matter must be established by the testimony of two or three witnesses" (2 Corinthians 13:1). To know if an implied insight is really true according to the Bible, look for another passage where the Bible says straight-out what you have seen implied in the first passage.

Where else, for example, does the Bible express directly that "no matter where we run, God is there''? (Psalm 139:1-12 expresses this truth very clearly!)

You're on solid ground, then, to match up *implied* insights from the Bible with *direct* statements of the same truth. The only problem is how to find those supporting Bible "witnesses." Sometimes you will just think of supporting passages because of what you already know about the Bible. Other times, you will need to use the cross-references in your Bible. Or look up the idea in a topical Bible.

Examples to Follow

What examples to follow can you find in Jonah 1?

After you have noted your own insights, check out the following suggestions for this *SPECS?* category:

(1) *God's love for Jonah, Nineveh, and the sailors* (vv. 1-2, 16-17).

(2) *Sailors' trying so hard to save Jonah* (vv. 8-13).

(3) *Ask questions before jumping to conclusions* (vv. 7-11).

(4) *Pray in a crisis* (vv. 5-6, 14). It's interesting that Jonah was commanded by the captain to get up and pray (v. 6), but there's no record in this chapter that he ever did. The sailors did all the praying in this situation.

(5) *God's mercy in providing a way of escape for Jonah* (v. 17).

(6) *The sailors feared God, offering sacrifices and vows to Him after He delivered them from near death* (v. 16).

(7) *Jonah's confession to the seamen that he was responsible for the mess they were in* (vv. 8-10).

Commands to Obey

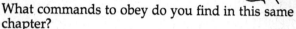

What commands to obey do you find in this same chapter?

You probably didn't find a lot of commands to obey. But here's at least one *implied* command: *God commanded Jonah to go to Nineveh* (vv. 1-2). *Likewise, we should be willing to go wherever, and do whatever, God leads.* Is the Lord speaking to you about something He wants you to do?

Stumbling Blocks to Avoid

Stumbling blocks are like warnings—things God wants us to watch out for. Can you find any of these in Jonah 1?

(NOTE: Sometimes an insight can be listed under the first "S" of "SPECS?" (sins) or the last "S" (stumbling blocks). The important thing is to get your insights down on paper. Don't worry about which "S" you place them under.)

Here are a couple of stumbling blocks to avoid which are implied in Jonah 1:

(1) *Never disregard circumstances as possible indicators that God is trying to get your attention.* A number of verses imply this warning: a. Jonah had to buy his own ticket to run away (v. 3). b. Violent storm on the sea (but not quite enough to break up the boat—v. 4). c. Captain's command to call on God (v. 6). d. The lot falling on Jonah as the culprit (v. 7). e. Questions the sailors asked of Jonah (vv. 8-11).

(2) *Never think your sin will only affect you.* Jonah's sin also hurt all the sailors. They lost their cargo and nearly lost their ship and their lives because of Jonah's sin (vv. 5, 11, 13-16).

?—The Big Question

The last *SPECS?* category is represented by a question mark. It's a reminder to end your time of meditation and application by asking, "Lord, what should I do now?"

A danger of using the *SPECS?* method is that we will see so much in a Bible passage that we won't know where to start applying the insights we've gained. There's also a subtle danger that in trying to apply a particular truth, we may fail to tackle an area which the Lord is more concerned about for us. It's possible to do good things as a substitute for the best.

That's why it's good to end a time of Bible meditation by asking the question, "Lord, what should I do now?" God is able to impress on you what is most important to Him for your life today.

Look back over Jonah chapter 1 and your list of *SPECS?* Ask the Lord to impress on you what is most important for you to work on this day.

As you commit yourself to obeying Him, remember what James has to say about wisdom: "If any of you lacks wisdom, he should ask God, who gives generously to all without finding fault, and it will be given to him" (James 1:5).

GOD GAVE THE BIBLE TO TEACH US WHAT TO
BELIEVE. BUT HE WANTS OUR BELIEFS TO MAKE
A DIFFERENCE IN OUR DAILY BEHAVIOR. THE
"WHOSE RESPONSIBILITY?" METHOD DESCRIBED
IN THIS CHAPTER CAN HELP THESE
TWO TRACKS MEET.

12

Who's Responsible?

"Why do I always get blamed for everything? It's not even my turn! I cleaned up the kitchen last night. It's Becky's turn tonight."

Sound familiar? It's never fun to be blamed for something that's not even your responsibility. God understands that. He gets blamed all the time for things that aren't His fault! How?

Have you ever prayed to become a better Christian, and nothing seemed to happen? Didn't God hear your prayer?

Yep. But the problem may be that you are blaming Him for something that's not His responsibility. He may be waiting for you to do *your* part.

There are some things only God can do, such as create new life and work miracles of healing. There are other things He can't (or at least won't) do for us, such as read our Bibles and pray.

It Takes Two

The Christian life works best when there is active cooperation between us and God. It doesn't work when we just kick back and "leave all the driving to Him." God will always do His part. The question is, will we do ours? In many cases, God waits to do His big part until we have done our little part.

If we are going to apply God's Word to our lives—and that is the ultimate goal of all Bible study—we must know clearly what He expects *us* to do. A meaningful way to study the Bible is to sort out what things God is supposed to do, His responsibility, and what things we are supposed to do, our responsibility.

Many parts of the Bible emphasize God's *commands* and the *blessings* that follow when we obey. Such passages come alive when analyzed in the light of what God asks us to do and what He in turn promises to do for us.

Let's Get Started

To begin, draw two vertical lines on a sheet of paper so the sheet is divided into three columns. Title the left column, "My Responsibility," and the right-hand column, "God's Responsibility." The middle column should be titled "Results or Miscellaneous." (See page 143.)

Pick a Bible passage and read it carefully, thinking about who is supposed to do what. As you read each verse, ask "What is here for God to do? What is here for me to do? Does the passage indicate what will be the result of either God or me doing our part?"

Rewrite each verse, dividing it among the three columns, according to where each part of the verse fits.

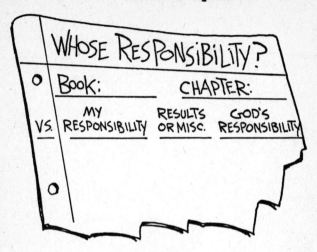

It Looks Like This

Psalm 119:1 in the *New International Version* reads, "Blessed are they whose ways are blameless, who walk according to the Law of the Lord." This verse tells us that we have two responsibilities. One is to keep our way blameless; the other is to walk in the Law of the Lord. Both would go in the "My Responsibility" column.

The same verse says that the one who does these two things is blessed. We can't bless ourselves; God has to bless us. So we would write "bless" under the "God's Responsibility" column.

The blessing also comes as a *result* of meeting our responsibilities (to keep our way blameless and to walk in the Law of the Lord). So "blessing" can also be written in the "Results" column. When part of a verse fits in more than one column, put it in both.

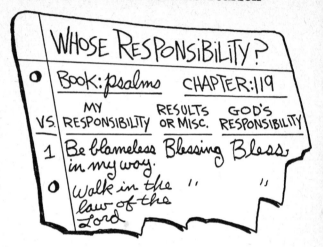

Use common sense as to what responsibilities are for us today. For example, suppose you read that David was supposed to bring a lamb to the tabernacle for a sacrifice. Don't write down that you are responsible to buy a plane ticket and a lamb and take it to Jerusalem for the next Sabbath! The "miscellaneous" category in the center column is for such information. Anything which can't clearly be assigned to God or us as responsibilities, or considered a result, should be put in the center section as miscellaneous information.

It's Your Turn

Try dividing up the next seven verses (vv. 2-8) of Psalm 119. Figure out *who's responsible to do what* in each of the verses before reading on in this chapter.

When you have finished, check out the chart on

page 146. If your chart doesn't look exactly like this one, don't worry. Some passages can be looked at in more than one way. (Notice also that not all verses contain something for all three columns.)

Were you surprised to see so few entries in the "God's Responsibility" column? People often think that most of the Bible is about what God is doing. But guess which column is usually the longest in this type of Bible study? You're right—"My Responsibility." The Bible is full of what God wants *us* to do!

Digging Deeper

You will find that dividing up eight verses using the "Whose Responsibility" method is about right for an average devotional period. Once you have made your entries into the three columns, here are two additional things you can do to maximize your spiritual profit from the passage:

First, **look up definitions of key words.** What would you select as the key words for the first few verses of Psalm 119? Perhaps "blessed," "blameless," "statutes," and "seek"? You can write a brief definition right by the word in one of the three columns.

We take so many words for granted because they sound familiar. We hear them often, but that doesn't guarantee we could give good definitions of them. God has spoken through *words*. To really understand what He has said, we have to understand what the words mean.

An English dictionary will help here. Even better is a Bible concordance which defines every word in the Bible. *Strong's* or *Young's* Bible concordances

"Whose Responsibility?"

Book **Psalms**   Chapter **119**   Verses **1-8**

VS.	My Responsibility	Results or Miscellaneous	God's Responsibility
1	Be blameless in my way Walk in the law of the Lord.	Blessing	Bless
2	Keep His statutes Seek Him with all my heart.	Blessing	Bless
3	Do nothing wrong Walk in His ways		
4	Fully obey His precepts		Lay down precepts
5	Pray that my ways may be stedfast to obey God's decrees		
6	Consider all God's commands	Not be put to shame	
7	Praise God with an upright heart Learn God's righteous laws		
8	Obey God's decrees		Not to utterly forsake me

are ideal for this purpose.

"But that sounds like work!" someone protests. "That takes careful thinking." Exactly. That's why it works. You are listening to God, thinking about what He's really saying, and deciding how to put His Word into practice.

A second way to dig deeper into "Whose Responsibility" is to **note any implications you see.** When we get a letter from a special somebody, we don't just read the words at face value and stop there. We read between the lines a lot of things he or she has *implied.*

Bible verses also contain implications—truths to be discovered "between the lines." For example, in Psalm 119:1, the following truth is implied: *To be able to walk in God's Law, we first have to know His Law.*

Write a Letter to God

Here's a third way to dig deeper in a "Whose Responsibility" study. Actually, this method can be used to follow up your "Whose Responsibility" findings, or by itself.

Did you ever stop to think that the Bible is a personal letter from God to you? God has written it to you to tell you about Himself and His plans, and about yourself and how you fit into His plans.

If Someone so important has written you such a long, loving, thoughtful letter, don't you think you ought to write back? A good way to respond to what God is saying to you in the Bible is to write a letter back to Him.

What do you say in a letter to God? Here are three main areas to write to Him about:

Thank You, Lord.

Help me, Lord.

I confess, Lord.

(Note the formation of the acrostic *THI*. You won't find *THI* in a dictionary! It's just a memory device.)

"Thank You, Lord." Start your letter by thanking Him for what He has written in His letter to you. Thank Him for what He has shown you about yourself, about Himself, and about your relationship with Him. Thank Him for what He has done, is doing, and has promised to do.

"Help me, Lord." You will often find that your "My Responsibility" column looks overwhelming. But fortunately the Christian life is not just doing what comes naturally. It's doing what comes supernaturally. No one can be successful at living the Christian life apart from the Lord's help. But His help is always available. Ask Him for it.

"I confess, Lord." Admit to the Lord any sin He has pointed out in your life. *Confession* is merely agreeing with what God says. You can write Him, asking forgiveness just as you might from a friend whom you have wronged.

Keeping in Touch

For practice, try writing one paragraph of thanks, one asking help, and one of confession. But don't worry about sticking to any special order.

On the following page is a letter that a teen wrote to God after sorting out *who is responsible* in Psalm 119:1-8. As you read the letter, notice how much it sounds like a typical letter to a friend.

One more word about writing letters to God—

Dear Lord,

The guy who wrote Psalm 119 really knew how important Your Word is. I don't think I'm quite as convinced as he was. If I were, I would study my Bible a whole lot more. Father, show me the importance of Your Word, and help me do what it says.

Thank You that, in the Bible, You promise to reward those who follow You. Those promises give me a little more incentive.

I want to mention something else. The author of Psalm 119 seemed to really enjoy Your Book. He must have spent a lot of his spare time reading it. (People usually don't enjoy homework assignments, but they do enjoy leisure-time activities.) I'd be a different person if more of my spare time was spent with You and Your Word.

I usually say, "Well, I've got to have my devotions now." But I bet that guy who wrote the Psalm would have said, "I <u>get</u> to have my devotions now!" Father, it is a privilege, not a duty, to study Your Word. Help me to see it that way.

With love,
Brian

keep the letters. Later, you can look back and see how He has answered them. And remember, regular correspondence helps build strong friendships. Stop reading now and write God a letter.

APPENDIX A

How to
Recognize Paragraphs

The following examples illustrate eight methods used in various Bible versions to indicate paragraph divisions.

1   Symbol ¶ Alone

3 But Jonah rose up to flee unto Tarshish from the presence of the Lord, and went down to Joppa; and he found a ship going to Tarshish: so he paid the fare thereof, and went down into it, to go with them unto Tarshish from the presence of the Lord. 4 ¶ But the Lord sent out a great wind into the sea, and there was a mighty tempest in the sea, so that the ship was like to be broken.   (Jonah 1:3-4)

2 Paragraph Titles Inserted

2 Arise, go to Nineveh, that great city, and cry against it; for their wickedness is come up before me.

The Prophet's flight from Jehovah;
the great storm.

3 But Jonah rose up to flee unto Tarshish from the

presence of the Lord, and went down to Joppa; and he found a ship going to Tarshish: so he paid the fare thereof, and went down into it, to go with them unto Tarshish from the presence of the Lord.
(Jonah 1:2-3)

3   Indentation

2 "Go to the great city of Nineveh, and give them this announcement from the Lord. 'I am going to destroy you, for your wickedness rises before me; it smells to highest heaven.'"

3 But Jonah was afraid to go and ran away from the Lord. He went down to the seacoast, to the port of Joppa, where he found a ship leaving for Tarshish. He bought a ticket, went on board, and climbed down into the dark hold of the ship to hide there from the Lord.   (Jonah 1:2, 3)

4   Bolder Print Verse Numbers

3 But Jonah rose up to flee to Tarshish from the presence of the Lord. So he went down to Joppa, found a ship which was going to Tarshish, paid the fare, and went down into it to go with them to Tarshish from the presence of the Lord.

4 And the Lord hurled a great wind on the sea and there was a great storm on the sea so that the ship was about to break up.   (Jonah 1:3-4)

5   Larger First Letters or Words at Start of Paragraph

THE Word of the Lord came to Jonah the son of

Amittai saying,

2 "Arise, go to Nineveh the great city, and cry against it, for their wickedness has come up before Me." (Jonah 1:1-2)

2 THEN JONAH PRAYED to the Lord his God from inside the fish:

2 "In my great trouble I cried to the Lord and He answered me; from the depths of death I called, and Lord, You heard me!" (Jonah 2:1-2)

6 Double Space Between Lines (Especially in Poetry)

11 Rescue me, and deliver me out of the hand of
  aliens.
Whose mouth speaketh deceit,
And whose right hand is a right hand of false-
  hood.

12 When our sons shall be as plants grown up in
  their youth,
And our daughters as cornerstones hewn after
  the fashion of a palace; (Jonah 2:11-12)

7 Paragraph Titles at Beginning of Chapter

CHAPTER 1

*Jonah, sent to Nineveh, flees to Tarshish: 4 He is over-
taken by a tempest, 11 Thrown into the sea, 17 And
swallowed by a great fish.*

NOW the Word of the Lord came unto Jonah the

son of Amittai, saying,
2 Arise, go to Nineveh, that great city, and cry
against it; for their wickedness is come up before
me.   (Jonah 1:1-2)

8   Symbol ¶ Plus
Paragraph Titles
Jonah flees from the Lord

2 Arise, go to Nineveh, that great city, and cry
against it; for their wickedness is come up before
me.
3 But Jonah rose up to flee . . . from the presence
of the Lord.
4 ¶ But the Lord sent out a great wind into the sea,
and there was a mighty tempest in the sea, so that
the ship was in danger of being broken.
                                       (Jonah 1:2-4)

APPENDIX B

Reference Books
for Bible Study

Books are listed in descending order of recommendation, both by categories and within categories.

1. **Bible Concordance**
   Strong, James H. *Strong's Exhaustive Concordance of the Bible*. Royal Publishers, 1890.
   Young, Robert. *Young's Analytical Concordance to the Bible*. William B. Eerdmans Publishing Company, 1955.

2. **Bible Dictionary**
   Unger, Merrill F. *Unger's Bible Dictionary*. Moody Press, 1957.
   Tenney, Merrill C., ed. *The Zondervan Pictorial Bible Dictionary*. Zondervan Publishing Company, 1970.

3. **English Dictionary**
   Woolf, H. Bosley, ed. *Webster's New Collegiate Dictionary*. Revised. Merriam Publishers, 1975.

4 Bible Commentary
Harrison, Everett F., and Pfeiffer, Charles F., eds. *Wycliffe Bible Commentary*. Moody Press, 1962.

5. Bible Handbook
Alexander, David and Patricia. *Eerdman's Handbook to the Bible*. William B. Eerdmans Publishing Company, 1973.

Halley, Henry H., ed. *Halley's Bible Handbook*. Revised. Zondervan Publishing Company, 1975.

6. Bible Atlas
Pfeiffer, Charles F. *Baker's Bible Atlas*. Baker Book House, 1961.

7. Bible Customs
Wight, Fred H. *Manners and Customs of Bible Times*. Moody Press, 1953.

8. Bible Introduction
Archer, Gleason L. *A Survey of Old Testament Introduction*. Moody Press, 1973.
Harrison, Everett F. *Introduction to the New Testament*. William B. Eerdmans Publishing Company, 1964.

APPENDIX C

Answers to Humorous Bible Questions in Chapter 9

1. Several possible answers:
   "Knee-high-miah" (Nehemiah—Nehemiah 1:1)
   Bildad the Shoe-height (Shuhite—Job 2:11)
2. Peter, the disciple who slept on his watch (Matthew 26:40)
3. Joseph, because Pharaoh made him into a ruler (Genesis 41:42-43)
4. When Joseph served in Pharaoh's court (implied in Genesis 41:38-46)
5. A little before Eve (Genesis 2:7, 21-22)
6. They raised Cain (Genesis 3:23; 4:1)
7. In Noah's ark (Genesis 7:13-23)
8. Job, because he had the most "patients" (patience—James 5:11)
9. Nick O'Demus (Nicodemus—John 3:1-5)

APPENDIX D

Answers to Jonah Crossword Puzzle (Chapter 9)

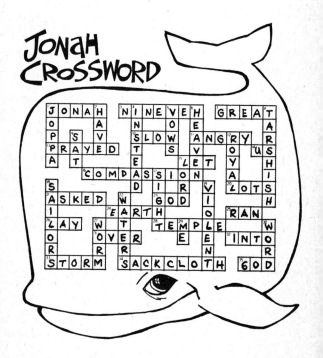

APPENDIX E

Scripture Passages for A Personal Memory Program

Passages Helpful in Sharing Your Faith
Fact of sin—Romans 3:23
Penalty of sin—Romans 6:23
Penalty paid by Christ—Romans 5:8
Salvation a free gift—Ephesians 2:8-9
Need of receiving Christ personally—John 1:12
Assurance of salvation—1 John 5:11-13

Passages Helpful in Facing Problems and Answering Questions
(Read the chapters cited and memorize the parts that are meaningful to you.)
Anxiety or worry—Matthew 6; Philippians 4; Psalm 37; 1 Peter 5
Assurance of salvation—1 John 5; Romans 8
Choosing a husband—Ephesians 5
Choosing a wife—Proverbs 31; 1 Peter 3
Critical spirit—1 Corinthians 13
Death of a loved one—1 Thessalonians 4; 1 Corinthians 15; John 14; Revelation 21; 22; Psalm 23

Depression—Psalm 42; Psalm 43
Doubt—James 1; Habakkuk
Family conflicts—James 4
Parents and children—Ephesians 6; Colossians 3
Fear—Psalm 121
Forgiveness of sin—1 John 1; Psalm 51
Fruitful life for Christ—John 15
God's will for you—Romans 12; 1 Corinthians 12;
   Ephesians 4
Guidance—Proverbs 3; James 1
Guilt—Psalm 103; Psalm 51
Hopelessness, helplessness—John 15;
   Philippians 4
Hunger for God's Word—Psalm 19; Psalm 119
Inferiority—Philippians 4; Psalm 139
Inability to sleep—Psalm 4
Joy—Colossians 3; Philippians 4
Love (true)—1 Corinthians 13
Parent problems—1 Peter 2
Physical illness—Psalms 6; 39; 41; James 5
Problems you didn't cause—Hebrews 12
Spirit-filled life—Romans 8
Success as a Christian—Matthew 5; 6; 7
Suffering, trials—2 Corinthians 1; James 1
Temptation—1 Corinthians 10; James 1
Victory over the old nature—Romans 6; 7; 8